Father Figures

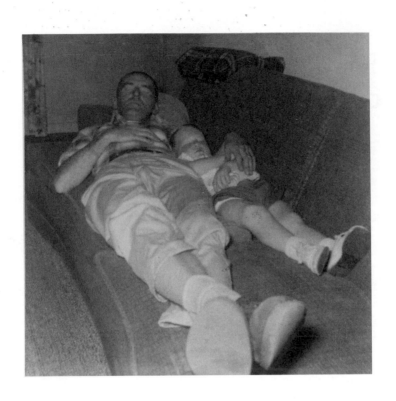

Father Figures

THREE WISE MEN WHO CHANGED A LIFE

Kevin Sweeney

ReganBooks

An Imprint of HarperCollins *Publishers*

HarperCollins books may be purchased for educational, business, or sales promotional use. For information please write: Special Markets Department, HarperCollins Publishers Inc., 10 East 53rd Street, New York, NY 10022.

FIRST EDITION

Designed by Kristi Norgaard

Printed on acid-free paper

Library of Congress Cataloging-in-Publication Data

Sweeney, Kevin, 1958–
    Father figures : three wise men who changed a life / Kevin Sweeney.
        p. cm.
    ISBN 0-06-051192-3
    1. Sweeney, Kevin, 1958—Childhood and youth. 2. Fathers and sons—California—San Bruno—Biography. 3. Father figures—California—San Bruno—Biography. 4. Sons—California—San Bruno—Biography. 5. San Bruno (Calif.)—Biography. I. Title.

HQ755.85.S92 2003
3116.874'2—dc21

2003041440

03   04   05   06   07   RRD   10   9   8   7   6   5   4   3   2   1

FOR JULIA SWEENEY AND
HANNAH KAYE

Contents

Foreword

In the year following the terrorist bombings of September 11, 2001, the *New York Times* ran a long series of obituaries, each offering a brief glimpse into the life of one of the victims. As I read, I was struck by the fact that so many were young men, in the prime of their lives, and that many of them left behind small children.

These personal stories had a familiar ring. My father, too, died in the prime of his life, and he left behind small children, six of them. I was three when he died.

The sadness embedded in the obituaries, many of them highlighted by the tiny details offered by loved ones, could at times be overwhelming. But I found myself reaching back to moments from my own childhood. Even as I mourned these deaths, I could recall that, though I was marked indelibly by a sad event, I did not have a sad childhood. I was a pretty happy kid.

This may have been because I did not feel fatherless, not exactly, even though my mother never remarried. I had a strategy for coping. I was a kid with a plan.

I shared these thoughts in an essay for Salon.com in the

autumn of 2001. I wrote hoping to help survivors see that their children might be resilient, even creative, in their grief. I wrote hoping to reach men in the communities where children had lost their fathers, because my own strategy for coping would not have worked were it not for the cooperation—in most cases, unknowing—of men in my hometown.

Several Salon.com readers wrote to tell me that their experiences mirrored mine. Some told me that they, too, had a strategy for coping; others wished they had found one. When they shared the details of their stories, though, very little of what was on the surface seemed to match what I had been through. What happened to each of us was different; much of what we felt was the same.

But the details had helped draw them out, helped them recall or reconsider what had happened in their own lives, or how they felt about what had happened. And this became another reason to write. The details, it turns out, are important.

1

Boom

"Your daddy has died," Grandma Fallon said. "Your daddy has died."

Four of us kids huddled together on the couch, still in our pajamas, with Grandma kneeling before us and clutching the folds of her dress. Staring at the floor, she said the words slowly, deliberately. We didn't say a thing.

Our sister Aileen was not on the couch with us, nor was she even in the room. She was alone in the hallway, standing over the heating vent—the dearest, most coveted spot in our house. With both slippers on the small floor register, she stood perfectly still as her nightgown billowed with our house's single strand of warmth. She was very tall for nine years and pretty, with long, straight red hair. Always the most capable one, on this morning when the house was filled with confusion, when something was happening, she withdrew to the one place of comfort, to that one place of perfection. But it came with a cost; she knew that right away. The warmth passed through my sister, through the thin sheet of a ceiling, through the attic, through the shingles and into a cold February. Though not in the room with her brothers and sisters, she had heard enough to know, but not enough to have actually been told. She was aware of this fact, that she was not present when the news of our father's death was announced. It was a useful distraction for a smart, young girl—a hurt that might obscure a death.

Aileen walked from the hallway, from the warmth and perfection she had found before Grandma had spoken, and into the front room. Terry was the one to tell her.

"Daddy died."

"Your daddy has died," Grandma said again. She was still looking down and began to cry quietly before us. We could not see her face, nor could we see her move at all, but teardrops fell onto her eyeglasses, pooled up, and rolled off the horn-rimmed edges to dampen her dress. It became a stream of giant teardrops, a flood, soaking folds in the fabric, changing its color. Terry cried and Pat cried. Anne and I stared at Grandma's dress.

Kathy was still off in her crib, in the room she shared with Pat and me. Fourteen months old and oblivious, probably, to everything except that she was wet, she was the only one who could breathe deeply enough to cry aloud, the only one to wail.

Everything I know from this day, and from this time, I know from my sister Terry, who was seven when Daddy died. I was too young—three and a half—and don't remember, but even the ones who were old enough don't remember. Terry is the one who held onto the details of our daddy, of our home back then, of how he died and of who did what and who went where after he died. If she is not the only one to remember, she is the only one to speak of it. Her memories have become mine.

All that happened back then, or all that we choose to remember, is part of the story of when Daddy died. Things can't be separated out now, nor can we consider the day and what happened without recalling the things that led up to it. The story is loaded with foreshadow, as if to suggest we should have known, even at that age, that it was coming. It feels so obvious in hindsight.

There were months and months of illness and fatigue. Daddy in the hospital with a bad heart. Daddy at home and too tired to pick us up. Whispering, only whispering, for days after Daddy is home from his first heart surgery.

Then there was the day, only two months before Daddy died, when the ambulance came to take our baby sister Kathy. It was at dinner a few days after Thanksgiving, and she was screaming and twisting, flailing around as if uncomfortable in every position. As Daddy held her on his lap, her neck grew stiff and her back arched. She began to stare straight ahead, a blank stare. Mom stood between the kitchen and dining room, talking on the phone to Dr. Bove, one hand on the receiver and one on her waist, her forehead leaning against the cabinets. That was when Pat shouted, "Mom, look at her eyes!" What we didn't know then was the word Mom had whispered to Daddy, the word Dr. Bove had used: meningitis. We did not know then— even Terry didn't know then—that our daddy's own little sister had died of meningitis long before, that it was all he could think of as the house was enveloped in Kathy's screams. We also didn't know then that a doctor had told our parents, only days earlier, that Daddy's heart was wearing out, that he needed rest for six to eight weeks so they could do more surgery, this time to open his heart and try new approaches not yet perfected. His fears, all so obvious in hindsight. The ambulance arrived before Mom finished up with the doctor—he must have been the one to call for it—and our baby sister was taken to the hospital. The spinal meningitis would not take our sister, not then or ever, but we were fated. "Bad things happen in threes," Grandma Sweeney had said so often. Daddy's surgery and the baby's meningitis. Something else would happen.

There was the day, two months later, when it snowed. Looking back, Terry could see why the two of them, Mom and Daddy, stayed inside that Sunday in January as we played outside in the snow. The doorbell had rung at six that morning, with Buzzy Flick, a neighbor from across the street, screaming "It's snowing, it's snowing!" It had never snowed before in San Bruno, which was new then, a tiny suburb on the peninsula south of San Francisco. Three inches of wet snow on the ground and we filed out of the house in the morning darkness, not knowing a thing about the cold and barely putting on sweaters. We built snowmen and forts, made massive stashes of snowballs, and raced inside because our fingers couldn't stand the cold, at least not right then. Our pew would be empty for 9:00 mass that day; Mom was afraid to drive in the snow, and besides, the Fanucchi kids built a snow wall and invited us to defend it against the

Garbans and all other comers. We ambushed anyone who moved and then took turns running inside to stand atop the heater or change clothes or cover our hands with heavy socks and plastic bags. We would stop in the living room to tell Mom and Daddy what was best about snow and how it was the greatest day and could they believe it? Daddy was in his plaid robe, with a T-shirt underneath. Under the T-shirt was the crisscross scar that reached all the way across his chest and onto his back. The two of them in the window, all day long, looking at us and at each other. Sometimes her hand was on his shoulder as he sat; sometimes they quietly held hands. In a few hours, after a night together in their bed, he would again go to the hospital. This time, he would not come home. Their last day at home together, alone with all that noise around them. Mom and Daddy in the window holding hands.

Then there was the day when we couldn't go inside the Stanford University Medical Center, where they could open a man's chest, even open a man's heart, fixing it and making him whole again. We stayed in the car in the semicircle driveway, with an auntie pointing up to a window, saying, "That's where your daddy is, in that room right there." Pointing to a window, any window. Five of the six kids outside in a car after an hour's drive, and they decided it was best not to bring us in. Perhaps we couldn't have known from looking at the window that they hadn't gotten it right, or it couldn't be gotten right. Perhaps our auntie knew and couldn't bear to bring us in.

Finally, there was the moment on the day Daddy died,

when the phone rang at six in the morning. A doctor told our mom that his condition had changed, that she should come quickly. She stood there again, between the kitchen and dining room, one hand on the receiver and one on her hip. Terry stood close to her, the seven-year-old observer, the listener, wondering why a call would come so early on a Thursday morning. Mom gave the detailed instructions. We were to wait until seven o'clock and then go fetch a neighbor. The neighbor was to pick up Grandma, who didn't drive, and bring her to our house to stay with us for a while. All of us were up now, except the baby, and Mom repeated the instructions, her tone suggesting we were big kids and would relish the opportunity to be on our own. Mom had to run off to see Daddy, and she pulled on her coat to make the drive to Stanford.

Fifteen minutes later, we pulled back the drapes and saw our mom, still on the sidewalk. She had driven all of a block, it turns out, when our car had failed—again—and she raced up the street on foot, checking to see who on the block might be awake. Now she was in front of the Flicks' house, pacing back and forth, frantic. Afraid to knock, afraid to wake the neighbors and trouble them yet again. Daddy's condition had changed and the car had died and the neighbors' drapes were all pulled shut. Shirley Flick emerged and, moments later, drove Mom to Stanford. Terry had seen enough to begin to feel real fear. Our mother confused and disheveled, in a heavy coat, pacing. This is when Terry knew.

Just a few minutes after Mom drove off with Shirley,

Grandma walked in the door. Someone had picked her up without our having to call. Some time later, perhaps an hour, perhaps more, the phone rang. Grandma stood in the same spot where Mom had stood, talking on the phone. We gathered around her, and that was when she ushered us to the couch.

"Your daddy has died," she said.

After we had heard and Aileen had heard, someone finally grabbed the baby to bring her to the front room. We were together, Jim and Marian Sweeney's six children, with our Grandma Fallon. We said very little.

Aileen left the room first, moving to the front door and gently touching the handle. She swiveled around, walked down the hallway to our parents' room, to the edge of their empty bed, leaning over the side closest to her. She did this several times, walking deliberately and whispering to herself. From the door to the bed and back again still. It would be many years before the rest of us would know she was counting the steps—the nineteen steps—from the front door to Mom and Daddy's bed. On the day he went into the hospital for the last time, the day after it snowed, Mom and Daddy stayed in bed together as the older children got ready for school. Aileen was rushing and shouted, "I'm leaving," as she walked out the door. She had no idea then that it would be his last day at home, the last day she would ever see him, and that "I'm leaving" would be her last words to her father. She had failed to take the nineteen steps to lean over the bed and kiss him. Only nineteen steps, but she left him there, lying in his bed. Her guilt was immediate and lasting. In the next ten years, Aileen would silently count those steps a thousand times, maybe ten thousand times. She had not kissed him or hugged him or whispered good-bye; she had failed at something that mattered. First she had her anger; now, she had her guilt, all in a span of half an hour. None of us knew how hard she took it. Aileen didn't even know.

———————————

Mom arrived at the hospital too late, as she somehow knew she would when she hung up the phone. And so my father died alone, at thirty-eight, of congestive heart failure. It was February 1, 1962.

My daddy, Jim Sweeney, was born in San Francisco in 1923, the first child of Irish immigrants. When he was twelve, he came down with strep throat. In those days, before penicillin, strep could develop into rheumatic fever, at least for the unlucky; my father, it turned out, was not lucky. He would survive the 106-degree fever, the swollen joints, the involuntary body movements, the lumps under the skin, and the red patches covering his body. But there was also the carditis, unnoticed at the time and unmentioned in the years after. An inflammation of the middle layer of heart muscle that coincides with rheumatic fever, it took a toll on Daddy's heart. The valves that once opened and closed efficiently had become screen doors with broken hinges, slamming shut or blowing open on a whim. He didn't know it, his parents didn't know it, and my mom didn't know it, but the poor kid was doomed. His fate cast at twelve, it was only a matter of time before his heart failed him.

I know little about my father's youth beyond his illness and the fact that meningitis killed one of his sisters. Those facts, plus the black-and-white photos with the formal poses, led me to see him as a serious boy. The brief hints about his young life, always said for the benefit of us children, suggested he was kind, brilliant, and thoughtful as a boy, and that as a young man he was dapper and a fabulous dancer. I believed this, if only half-heartedly, but knew the part about his dancing was true from the way Mom said it. My father was a great dancer. He loved to dance.

He was popular in San Bruno, something I knew to be true because it was written in the *San Bruno Herald,* in Daddy's obituary. The director of the funeral home was quoted as saying the crowd for the wake was "extraordinary," with large numbers waiting outside before getting a chance to come in and pay their respects. I read the clipping, tucked at the bottom of one of Mom's drawers, many times as a boy.

He sailed the Pacific during World War II, serving as a radioman on a navy cruiser, the *USS Columbus.* As a civilian, he held a variety of jobs and, for many years, helped run the Dye-Dee-Wash Diaper Service. At times, he collected soiled rags and delivered fresh ones driving a truck which played "Rock-a-Bye Baby," but mostly he worked in the office—he was in management. His career path held to a steady downward arc, something I didn't learn until decades after his death. Always able to find jobs, he was also able to lose them. He left the diaper service a few years before his death, and his last job was as a city maintenance worker—he drove the street sweeper in the autumn when San Bruno's sycamores and Chinese elms littered the ground with leaves.

My mother was also a San Franciscan and the eldest child of Irish immigrants. She took secretarial jobs after graduating from high school, and her first job was in the offices of the JC Penney store downtown, where she worked for a man who chewed tobacco but rarely hit the spittoon when he spat. She played tennis often as a girl and claims not to have been very serious about much of anything while growing up.

I do know she was serious about her friendships, and she remains so. When we were growing up, her friends from the first grade at St. Cecilia's Catholic School seemed a constant presence at our home. Seven girls—Dolores Kelly, Alice Gaffney, Carm Rea, Virginia Acton, Helen Barry, Noel Callaghan, and our mom, Marian Sweeney—would be friends from their sixth year until their last. The clique of little girls would become a clique of elderly women. When Daddy died, the St. Cecilia's girls repaid our mom for her loyalty; they were like sisters to her, like aunts to us. Even as kids, we could see that lifelong friendships, or the people who held them, were special. We felt closer to these women—and to their husbands and families—than to others of our parents' friends. They had known all of us kids all of our lives, and perhaps we understood, even then, that we would stay in touch with them, at least once or twice a year, for the rest of their lives.

In San Bruno, people loved our mom. She was a mom other kids wanted to talk to, a mom other parents turned to for advice.

Our mom had been told repeatedly that her husband could die, that the surgery was dangerous, that the problem revealed when he applied for a home insurance policy was indeed a serious one. But she could not hear the words. Given the size of our family and the size of our house—polar opposites—it's no wonder she couldn't hear. Or maybe it was just that the words were incomprehensible, or that the implications were too great to consider. And so, despite the fact that my father suffered from a long illness, his death was a complete shock, to his wife and to his children. There is not a single photograph of our whole family together—Mom, Daddy, and their six kids—that's how sudden it was. Boom. Daddy is dead.

Marian Sweeney was now a thirty-four-year-old widow with six children. Pat, the oldest child, was ten. Aileen was nine, Terry was seven, and Anne was six. I was three and a half, and Kathy, the baby, was fourteen months old. Our mom, already tired from the illnesses, was unprepared and afraid. She was also broke.

My parents had no savings whatsoever; we were already poor when he died, a big family crammed into a small house. My brother remembers a series of bicycles that he used or owned, always wondering if the bike would break down on the way to a game or practice. Our car broke down, our bikes broke down, and that was all before Daddy died. Things could only get worse with the loss of the one income in a one-income family. And, in the months after Daddy's death, a string of debts emerged from the woodwork.

The bills and paperwork were overwhelming, and they needed to be dealt with immediately. Uncle Roger, Daddy's younger brother, walked Mom through the process of making the death official, waiting with her at the Social Security Administration, the Veterans' Administration, the county clerk's office, and all the other places where they wanted proof that her husband was no more. Roger, a fireman, taller and louder than any of the Sweeney men, stood quietly in each line with my mom, his arm draped gently on her shoulder. He was the funniest and most lively man in our world, and it was a revelation to see him at the dining room table with our mom as she plodded through her piles of bills and papers. He was serious and silent with our mom, though he broke away occasionally to wrestle or tickle or read half a book to us. The forays were short, though; the bills were overwhelming.

There was no privacy in our house, so it was all out in the open—right there on the dining room table. We saw the piles of bills and heard the whispers. And so our mom called a family meeting, with all of her children except the baby, to explain our finances. I could barely count, and couldn't yet add, but was included. Pat was the one who finally asked the question that mattered most.

"Mom, how are we going to live? Who will take care of us?"

"Uncle Sam is going to take care of us," she said. "And we are so lucky."

We didn't feel particularly lucky about any of this, certainly not right then, but it turned out that our new uncle would indeed deliver. The first of his big green checks would take several months to arrive, but Mom at least knew what the monthly allotment would be. It would get us through, barely, at least for a while. Our mother told us with absolute certainty that our government would help us, and it did; over time, this would offer a sense of bedrock. I don't recall the family meeting—both Terry and Mom remember it clearly—but as I look back, it seems to have had an impact not unlike that of an imprint.

The money situation, though unfortunate, could at least be figured out. It was simple arithmetic, with sums and debits and knowable answers. Everything else was complicated, including what to do with the children.

In the immediate days after Daddy's death, the older kids were farmed out to other families, mostly to give our mom a chance to rest and to grieve. Decisions made casually, they may have been more important than Mom imagined. Aileen, so harsh in her own judgment of herself, spent several nights with a Norwegian family on Sycamore Avenue. Well-meaning and exceedingly gentle, they were taciturn and could never have coaxed her into discussions of her guilt, even if they had seen the need. Terry went to the Ranneys, and Pat Ranney was the only Irish woman we knew who hugged, who really hugged, even people outside of her family. Mrs. Ranney sat on the bed to talk with Terry, asking about her hurt and her sadness and her recollections of Daddy. Terry may have been the only one of us to talk aloud about Daddy during that time, which may be why we rely on her memories today. I don't know which house Pat or Anne went to, though I know Kathy and I stayed at home, where we were held constantly by our aunts, our neighbors, and Mom's St. Cecilia's friends.

We viewed our daddy's body at the funeral home, all six of us children together and with no one else in the room except our mother and Pat Ranney. There were many who told Mom that the younger children should be kept from the funeral—the public events would be too sad, they said, too overwhelming—and she acquiesced. Of course, sadness was what we had; we couldn't be spared. Barring the youngest kids from the services only gave us access to the complicating feelings of jealousy and anger—the older kids got to go and we didn't. Perhaps we would have wailed, perhaps not. But our chance to say good-bye—or at least our chance to see the range of emotions people might show as they say good-bye—was snatched from us. We were let loose on that field where competing emotions are present but camouflaged.

After the burial—where the rifle salute caused Auntie Anne, fragile from her brother's death, to jump so quickly that her hat fell to the ground—our mom received unsolicited direction from a priest at St. Robert's.

"I'll give you two pieces of advice, Marian." He spoke with great confidence and an air of formality. "First, don't wear black. The children don't need to see that. And second, I want you to have that smile on your face that you always have. I want you to come to church that way and let the people see what you can do."

We were not to show sadness. And our right to cry in church, of all places, was taken. That was his decree, and it became our family's strategy. He may have thought feelings of sadness could be willed away with a chosen facial expression. He may have known that being an approachable widow could lead to a more sympathetic reception from the parish, to greater support from the flock. More likely, it may simply be that this is what people did back then—it was how they dealt with death in 1962. My mother had no choice, really, in whether or not to take this path; a thousand years of Irish Christendom made it inevitable that she would heed the advice of her priest. And so, in the whole of my youth, I don't recall a single instance when anyone, in my family or outside of it, asked me what I remembered of my father, if I missed him, or how I felt about his absence. When no one asked, I forgot what I knew. By the time I asked myself, I could no longer find within me what I might have felt, or might be feeling, really, about his death.

It would be seventeen and a half years—the summer of 1979—before we would talk, as a family, about our sadness.

2

There's My Boy

Our house, on Cypress Avenue, had three bedrooms. One was our mother's, and though she slept in it by herself, she continued to share it with our father. The left half of the closet would remain nearly empty for a long, long time, nearly all of Daddy's clothes having been given away in the weeks after his death. I can remember only two things ever hanging on that side: a bowling shirt with the name "Lovey" embroidered on the front, and the pale blue tie Lovey wore the day he married Mom. Empty, but warm and safe, Daddy's half of the closet was a good place to hide during games. It felt natural to hide in the very hole that sent me searching. Mom had a wide, low dresser that had also been shared. The right side had been his and was now filled with files, papers, and family keepsakes. The hope chest contained, still, many of the dresses Mom wore on her honeymoon. It was off-limits, because its contents were both dear and fragile, but when I was five, I opened it often to touch the neatly folded flag that had draped Daddy's coffin. I held it in the way I had seen John-John Kennedy do so on television when his own daddy, the president, had been shot and killed. It was my daddy's flag, given for service to his country.

The three older girls—Aileen, Terry, and Anne—shared a room. A bunk bed, another twin bed, and one dresser took up most of the space. Toys were piled on the ends of the beds or under them. Every inch of the closet was crammed, mostly because that might pass for clean: If the room looked clean, it was clean. It was a corner room with two windows, full of light and breezes and the sound of jets taking off from the airport nearby.

Pat and I shared a room with Kathy. Pat had the top bunk, I had the lower. Kathy used a crib at first, then a twin bed. Ours was the smallest room in the house, but two of us were the smallest kids, so it seemed about right. As my ten-year-old brother hit twelve, thirteen, fourteen, we would fill it to bursting. Except for a few days a year, our room was always sloppy, with toys and clothes and scraps of Pat's homework pushed under the bed or stuffed into piles in the corner. The crowding demanded one extreme or the other: absolute spotlessness or just making space to walk through. We chose the latter, though I don't know if we were ever aware that the other extreme really existed. There were no empty spaces in our room, or anywhere else in the house for that matter. We were packed in.

A hallway ran down the middle of our house. On one side were the bedroom doors; on the other was the long wall shared by the living room, and it held the house's only heating vent. One by one, we would wake ourselves in the morning, starting the day by standing over the vent. If there were two of us, one would stand over the hall side and the other over the living room side, and we could talk to each other easily through the vent. If both sides were taken, I would lie in bed until one spot opened up, then bolt to a vent as it became available. For roughly half the year, standing over the heater was the first thing we did in the morning and the last thing we did at night.

The heating vent also provided rare access to the world of adults, where our circumstances were frequently a topic of conversation. If adults were visiting Mom in the living room, there would be at least one of us listening through the vent to the whispered conversation. Always. At five, this is how I learned that our family was poorer than others, and how I learned that others respected my mom in ways that surprised even them. Boasting was never allowed in our home—the sin of pride was considered a grand one—so we never heard Mom talk about how she managed to survive with so little. When her friends would utter the magical phrase, "I don't know how you do it," I would be full of admiration for my mom, for her skill and her competence, for the fact that she stood out. In the evenings, Pat and Aileen played traffic cop at the heating vent. There were times when they waved me off, indicating that it was a conversation they could eavesdrop in on, but that I could not. I believed they were protecting me, that there were things young children should not hear, and I trusted them. Pat was the oldest boy, the man of the house now, and Aileen was making up for what she had seen as her past failures, a young girl already seeking atonement. The two of them assumed the role of parent before they were even teenagers, together trying to make up for the absence of our daddy. While it may have taken a toll on them, I benefited greatly.

The kitchen was our house's other warm room. The gas stove was always warm to the touch, and we pressed our backsides against the oven door while hovering about Mom or waiting for an empty surface on which to make our lunch. Some nights, she put our pajamas in the oven for a few moments before bedtime. We slid them on just as soon as she removed them, when they were more hot than warm. There was no better feeling, we thought, and no better mom. She was pretty, she was fun, and she baked our pajamas when it was cold.

The bathroom was always occupied. Like a bird feeder in the middle of an estate garden, there was always someone in it or at it, always someone pushing to get in.

———————————

Before we started school, Kathy and I were portable, and we stayed for days at a time with Grandma and Grandpa Sweeney in San Francisco. They picked us up in their old Rambler, which Grandpa, then in his late seventies, drove slowly and carefully, as if it were made of balsa wood held together with craft glue. He gripped the wheel with both hands and turned the car methodically, one hand over the other. When other cars neared, and sometimes when they didn't, Grandma would shout, "Jim! Watch out for the machine!" No one else's grandmother used the word *machine* for a car, not in California, not anywhere. We made fun of her for it—all of our cousins did as well—though never to Grandma's face. Tiny, pretend wives would scream the phrase as we pushed little Matchbox cars from the dining room table or off the front porch. The plastic cover on the Rambler's back seat had bumps and ridges to stop children from sliding as the car turned; it provided no such use for us—Grandpa's turns were always slow—but left patterns on our legs that looked, at least in the presence of our grandparents, like crosses.

Grandma and Grandpa Sweeney's house was where our father grew up and was filled with relics that proved his existence. There was his first Holy Communion picture on the dresser, a white cloth draped over his arm. Two framed photos showed his sister, Maureen, and him playing with a dollhouse, which was still right there in the basement. When Kathy and I played with the dollhouse, which was often, it was rarely a game of dolls; instead, we played Jimmy and Maureen. Other clues and memories lurked in the house on Holloway Avenue, but we had to find them on our own, without hints. Grandma's sadness was overbearing, a showy grief that demanded attention to itself, so it was too risky to ask her about Daddy; the mention of his name caused her lips to quiver. So we rooted around in the basement and the downstairs bedroom, the room that had once been his. Early one morning, I pulled the heavy drawers out of his dresser to see if any of his notes or papers had slipped behind. Looking for a note from my father.

I loved going to their house. I loved getting up late at night to examine Grandpa's false teeth on the bathroom sink. I loved the soda bread Grandma made, and the way she kneaded it mercilessly on the kitchen table. The older kids knew then that Grandma served real butter, and they smothered her bread with it.

Grandma Sweeney was stern, raised on Inishmaan, one of the tiny Aran Islands, twenty miles off Ireland's west coast. Whatever North Atlantic storms she weathered as a child on that tiny rock still brewed within her, leaving her calloused and, at times, cold. Though she forgave, she could also take on an unforgiving air. When my sister Terry was born, she was the second female granddaughter, and the second one to not be named Mary, which was Grandma's name. (Mary was my sister's middle name, however.) Grandma took to bed for weeks after the birth, attempting, perhaps, to show how great the insult had been. She insisted on calling my sister *Theresa Mary,* because there was no saint *Terry,* and calling a child by a name other than a real saint's name was condemnation. Apparently, this rule only applied to girls, as no saint bears the name *Jim* or *Jimmy,* the names she used to call her husband and son. But I was a boy, and boys were spared any of this; Grandma clearly favored boys over girls. I knew Grandma respected me. I loved her because she was smart and had a fondness for good jokes and stories. I also loved her for her crisp accent, for her brilliant use of words and facial expressions, and for the way she spoke of the old country. I may even have loved her for the sadness embedded in all those wrinkles on her face and hands. As a young girl, she had been stricken by skeletal tuberculosis. To stem the disease, her left kneecap was removed, and she could never again bend that leg. It made for dramatic gestures in church when it was time to kneel: She shoved her bad leg straight under the pew in front of her, balancing all of her weight on the good leg. At home, she went up and down the curved wooden staircase like Ahab, with a clop, step, clop, step that would serve as warning if we were into things best left alone. Her bad knee made it possible for us to inspect every square inch of the downstairs. When her square black heel hit the top step, we closed the books, pushed in the drawers, poured the coins back into the jars, and folded Daddy's sailor shirt.

Our grandpa was warm and gentle, at least in his treatment of us. Long before we were born, he owned a bar and rooming house for sailors, had been a longshoreman on San Francisco's docks, and was a heavy drinker, so his gentleness may have been a gift to him in his old age. He called me "boy," and said, "Well, well, well, there's my boy now," as he walked up the steps of our house for a visit. He shook my hand—at five, I thought his hands were massive—and gave me his hat to carry in and place on the mantel. I loaded his pipe for him, taking in the sweet smell and sitting on his lap as he lit it. The flame from the wooden match was drawn down into the bowl, into the tobacco, then wafted upward in a shoot of smoke and fire as he exhaled. Over and over, the flame went down, then up, as he lit the pipe; if he lit his pipe in the basement, the room went light then dark, light then dark, as if a flashing neon sign were mounted just outside the window. His face always had stubble, and I brushed my soft cheek against his. I could stare at his ears for minutes, mesmerized by the thick, dark shorthairs, and reached in occasionally with a tiny finger to tickle him.

He escaped Grandma, and perhaps other things, perhaps even the deaths of two of his children, by puttering around in the garage, and I was always welcome there. He had a wall full of hand tools—drills, planers, and saws with worn wooden handles. He used his tools slowly and carefully, showing me some of the good a man could do with his hands. I learned less about how to use the tools than I did about how Grandpa used the tools. He was more interesting to me than the wall full of instruments. When I was five, Santa gave an older sister a plastic Barbie bed, but on Christmas afternoon, one of us stepped on the toy and shattered it. As I sat with Grandpa at his workbench later that week, he let me slowly and carefully sand the edges of pine two-by-fours, which, after Mom sewed covers for them, became Barbie beds and couches. With Mom's help, he turned an old drawer into a lined closet. They were the simplest of toys, made lovingly by our grandpa. With his simple gifts, my sisters now had Shaker Barbies.

He and I walked for hours each day, holding hands as we wound through San Francisco fog. His leather shoes cracked on the moist sidewalks, a sound I hoped for, but never found, in every pair of shoes I had during childhood. He often mumbled "The Foggy Dew," an Irish revolutionary song, as we walked. At the time, I figured he didn't know the words, because he mumbled through parts, as a scat singer would. Years later, when I learned the words, I assumed he avoided the mention of dying soldiers intentionally.

As much as I loved staying at their house, it came with a price. Every night at seven, we knelt together to say the rosary. We said the full rosary—every last word. The Apostles' Creed to start, and the Our Father and Glory Be to the Father before each decade. We recited these decades of rosaries in named bunches; there were five sorrowful decades, five joyful decades, and five glorious ones. Though there was logic connecting certain decades with specific days of the week—Sundays were supposed to be a glorious day, for example—it still seemed as if Grandma chose the sorrowful decades and their woes by habit. The agony, scourging, crowning by thorns, carrying, and crucifixion somehow seemed to make her more comfortable than the visitation, the nativity, or the ascension. It fit with the quivering lips. It was endless, but we were grateful that the process was hurried by Grandpa, who started the Hail Mary long before the Holy Mary was finished. Then Grandma called the saints, one by one, with the rest of us answering, over and over, "Pray for us." Some nights, we prayed along with Father Peyton, who led the Rosary Crusade, and who could be heard nightly on the Mutual Radio Network, his monotone alternating between praising Mary and begging her help. If Father Peyton was on, we were in for it; he knew more saint names than Grandma did. By the time he was finished, the phrase "Pray for us" had been wrung dry of any thought or feeling.

My visits there were about many things, including a

glimpse at my father's life. But mostly, I wanted to be around Grandpa. There were enough women and girls in our family, and I needed something different. I watched how he walked, how he licked his fingers before turning the pages of the newspaper, how he could sit so very still for so very long. I didn't know what I was looking for, but he was my father's father, and I knew that part of what I needed was there inside him. If Grandpa was in the room, I couldn't take my eyes off of him. I felt a satisfaction every time he spoke to me, every time he said, "There's my boy now."

Our family was huge. I had many aunties, uncles, and cousins who lived close by—and there were dozens more, hundreds more, in Ireland. Our gatherings at Christmas and Easter, for anniversaries and birthdays, were great fun. Our aunties were warm and generous with their time—Daddy's sister Maureen took the four eldest to Disneyland once and was always taking one or two of us for outings in San Francisco. The uncles teased us and played games with us in the street.

Our family was also extended, in particular by Mom's circle of friends. We had massive picnics in city and county parks— four or five moms, a few dads, and three dozen kids running around. Each of us had our favorite among the St. Cecilia clique, though the two women who had remained single gave and received the most attention. Helen, the sweetest, was Kathy's godmother, and generally acknowledged in our home as Kathy's personal property. Noel, the smartest, was the one I hovered about the most.

When any of the husbands of these St. Cecilia's girls were around, I followed them like a baby duckling. Chick Kelly, a butcher, was the only dad in the group we saw as often on his own as we did with his wife, Dolores. Stopping by to bring string-tied, white paper packages filled with meat, he would stay, for half an hour or more, sitting still at our dining room table talking to our mom. He would turn slowly, with a smile and a raised eyebrow, as I approached the table, asking me what I was up to. Jim Gaffney, tall and lean, filled our living room, our house even, when he came to pick up Alice. Both men commanded respect and interest without saying a word. I loved it when they visited. I sought them out when we stopped by their homes for a family visit.

On that Christmas of the broken Barbie bed, the younger kids learned that our brother Pat was a god. He wasn't *the* God, of course, not the God who could have explained things. But he was *our* god, and our lives were shaped by the fact that he was a generous one. Not long after Daddy died, Pat had taken on a paper route, delivering the news to ninety houses every afternoon except Sunday. Thanks to the *San Mateo Times* and the big tippers down on Linden Avenue, he had money in his pocket. At the age of twelve, he went on the first of many Christmastime gift-buying binges. I can't remember what he bought the girls—I didn't care—but there was a tommy gun under the tree for me and my brother Pat had put it there. I shot a million rounds on that gun, knocked over hundreds of banks, and used it for protection while selling millions of gallons of bootleg whiskey.

Pat was the only one of us kids who knew we had been poor before Daddy died, before we had a decent excuse. The first new baseball mitt he ever had was the one he bought for himself. Each year, everything he earned during two full months of deliveries would be used to spare us the same fate. He bought us toys, supplementing the ones Mom had purchased, and he only bought new ones.

He settled disputes, reprimanded us when we were at fault, and rewarded us for good behavior. He occasionally even demanded that we refer to him as God, though he generally used his power judiciously. He teased and tickled and could burn the skin on my wrist by grabbing it just so. He played games with us, endless board games, ball games, and word games. He was as smart and as fun and as generous as an uncle. He did more than pick up the tab: He set the tone. Because he came first, our mother never had to encourage us to share.

3
Wally Bunker Day

A few days after my sixth birthday, I was enrolled in St. Robert's Catholic School. There were five of us Sweeneys in the school's eight classrooms, a presence we were proud of, but our wake was not the widest, not by a long shot. The Monaghans, Cilias, Spachers and Voreyers all had bigger families, and each had a child in my class. Being the fifth child in a family at St. Robert's was as close as I'll ever come to experiencing life in a caste system. Even before we arrived on that first day, Sister Theophane, the Franciscan nun who taught my older siblings to read, knew how to handle each child from the big families. She knew in advance if we were smart or dumb, if we were hellion or angel, if we could follow along or not. She treated all kids respectfully, but she also treated me in ways that showed she assumed I was smart and, if not angelic, at least helpful. My sister Anne, who preceded me directly, was a perfect student, the brightest among us and never disruptive, so when I misbehaved, Sister assumed it was a momentary thing. Anne also was someone who could have friends of different ages—a classic bridge-builder of a middle child—and she could step in to make sure I was never alone on the playground. By the end of that first year in school, I knew that so much in my life might have been utterly different if my older siblings had been jerks.

One day that year, I walked out of school after the three o'clock bell to find Uncle Roger waiting, leaning against his shiny red Chevy Nova. Whenever we drove with him, he told us the car was loaded with fire equipment and that we weren't to touch the buttons on the dashboard—one was for a siren, one for a ladder in the trunk, and the other would vary, depending on his mood. On that day, he waited for all five of the Sweeneys then at St. Robert's and took us straight to Shaw's Ice Cream Parlor. Before homework, before dinner, before anything else. As we piled into his car, heading off for fresh dipped cones, our friends were jealous of us, making the experience even better. I don't know how often Uncle Roger did this—I know he did it several times when we were little—but the first time was a moment of enlightenment. It confirmed our sense that every so often really good things would happen to us. We were not forlorn kids; people were looking out for us. Other kids could even be jealous of us.

I remember doing artwork in class one day, when the girl sitting behind me took two paces forward, and vomited on my desk. It appeared to me that it was a deliberate act, but the poor kid had just barfed, and even I could find no way to shift the attention from her sickness to my own status as victim. Sister Theophane relied on her stash of prior impressions formed over the years. I was a Sweeney, and Sweeneys were helpful, so she suggested without a hint of sympathy or irony that I clean it up. I went to the supply cabinet in the hallway, grabbed the can of scented green sawdust, and sprinkled some on my desk and more on the floor. As the sawdust soaked up the girl's breakfast, I wiped it off the desk. I swept the floor and neatly filled the class pail, which I took outside to empty into the larger waste container in the play yard. I did all of this without instruction or suggestion, and Sister continued pacing around the classroom, making sure the students paid attention to their work and not to the boy janitor. For the remainder of the year, when a child vomited, I was the one to clean it. It was vomit, but I liked that I was a resourceful first grader, that I was a kid who could get a job done.

Sister Theophane was scary and firm, not the kind of teacher children loved, even first graders. But she loved sports, like all the nuns at our school, and she wheeled in a television set so we could watch World Series games. She told us stories about Wally Bunker, another six-year-old boy she had taught to read. Only five years after graduating from St. Robert's, Wally, at the age of nineteen, was pitching in the major leagues for the Baltimore Orioles. He threw his blistering fastballs—the ones his dad had taught him right there in San Bruno Park—and in his first full year in the majors, he won nineteen games, lost only four, and threw two one-hitters. He was, as the baseball scouts would say, a *phee-nom,* and a million American boys wanted to be him. But when I was in first grade, he was still just ours. He was our guy, and he was coming back to St. Robert's.

We took half a day to prepare for Wally Bunker Day, cleaning our classroom, and making pennants with his name on them. Half were blue and red, the St. Robert's colors; half were orange and black, the colors of an Oriole cap. These we taped to our rulers and waved as he drove up Oak Avenue in his Avanti sports car. He was so big, it seemed like he could barely fit through the doors. But he managed, and he came and went in a flash. Later that day, Sister Theophane pulled me out of the classroom. She warned that what she was about to tell me was something I could not tell any of the other boys, because they would be very jealous. I gave my word that I would not, a promise she knew I would keep—she had that much confidence in her power.

"Kevin Sweeney," she said, looking right into my eyes. "Do you know who sat in the very seat you're sitting in today?"

"No, Sister, I do not," I answered, barely able to breathe and afraid to ask who.

"Wally Bunker did."

She said nothing more, and didn't have to. A wrinkled nun in her sixties had found the right thing to say, the right way to tell me that I could do anything I wanted to. It wasn't until the eighth grade that I discovered she said the same thing to many boys that week. By then, her work was done: She had allowed me to have an ego. Boasting or talking about oneself could still draw a reprimand, at St. Robert's and at home, but it was okay to believe, okay to know you could do great things.

Wally began having arm troubles his second full year in the

major leagues, and his injuries kept him from meeting the potential he showed as a rookie. But in 1966, when I was a third grader, he won four crucial games in September, as the Orioles made a successful run at the American League pennant. He earned the right to pitch in the World Series. And he was magnificent, becoming only the sixth player ever to pitch a complete game, 1-0 shutout victory in the World Series. It was a day when our town stood still. Absolutely still. It was our brush with greatness. I would think of this day often as I rode my bike past his family's house, just six blocks from our own. A kid from St. Robert's could do great things, even if the breaks went against him.

Pat was in the eighth grade when I was in first, the only year we attended school together. It was also the last year he would play so direct a role in my life—his high school was ten miles away, his days became full and he held jobs into the evening. But he was still the man of the house. He was the one I looked up to. All of us did.

In any chore he did, I was his apprentice. He showed me how to mow lawns, first cutting in one direction, giving it a rake, then cutting with the mower pushed in another direction. The job wasn't finished until the edges were clipped and the sidewalk swept. A lawn should look perfect when it's done, like the field in a baseball stadium.

Because his paper route was so big, and because the papers needed delivering by 5:00 in the evening, he gave me fifteen houses to deliver—all the houses on our block and on Sycamore. They were mine to deliver, these houses, all on my own and every day but Sunday. He taught me to fold the papers with the company name facing out—so customers would know it was the *San Mateo Times* and not a throwaway. He taught me how to carry the papers efficiently, so the weight was balanced on my shoulders. He took me with him in the evenings as he made monthly collection rounds, knocking on doors and asking people to pay up.

"Collecting for the *Times,*" he would say.

He paid me ten cents a day and let me keep the tips from my houses, but when we stopped at Zanetti's Liquors for a treat, the sodas and beef jerky were always on Pat. I was a first grader, barely more than four feet tall—making good money. It was a responsibility and an occasional burden, but I was the only kid my age who could brag about his job. And now, like my brother, I had change in my pocket.

At the end of my first-grade year, Sister Theophane had us do one last art project. We each traced the bottom of our shoe onto several pieces of colored construction paper. We were making Father's Day presents, and the card was to say "On top of my sole, Dad, I love you." I had no father, of course, and our family no longer celebrated Father's Day, but the project was something the entire class would do.

"You have a grandfather, still, and uncles," Sister said. "You should make it for one of them."

What she proposed felt too awkward, too much like a request, and I was unwilling to ask for the kind of attention a dad might give. But I finished the project and turned in the shoe-shaped card of green, red, and blue paper. I had printed, in thick black pencil, "On top of my sole, Pat, I love you." It was the only time in my childhood that I recall telling anyone that I loved them, either out loud or in writing. It was not a phrase we used, and if I could not say it out loud, it at least felt natural to write it. It was Father's Day, and Pat was who we had.

That summer, before Pat started off to high school and before I started the second grade, he let me apprentice on another kind of job. It involved a neighborhood rite of passage, at least for the boys on our street, and it was far too dangerous for a boy not yet seven. But Pat knew it was something I would learn about anyway, so he took the lead in teaching me.

4

Big Green Checks

In the summer before second grade, I followed in my brother's footsteps as a collector and trader of gunpowder.

We lived three hundred yards from what was then a United States Navy operations base, a landlocked center where administrators arranged for the worldwide transport of supplies. Rows of offices and barracks marked one end of the base; the other end was open space, roughly one square mile of it, filled with grasses, cottonwoods, eucalyptus groves, and a creek.

Every few weeks, we heard the wonderful sound of gunshots from the wooded areas and creek beds, hundreds of rounds over several hours. They were battle exercises, or "practice wars," as we called them. Young marines and sailors hid in bushes, put their heads up long enough to take aim and fire, to grow accustomed to the noise of war. Those sounds started a gathering of boys on our street, and as they trailed off, we watched the clock: Our parents insisted that we stay on our side of the four-lane for a full hour after the last gunshot. Then we raced across, fanning out over the base in teams to search for battlefield spoils.

Those able to find what had just been a soldier's hideout would likely find a cache of spent shotgun shells. The shells had once been filled with gunpowder, which gave the shot the proper sound and kick, but the tips never contained anything deadly, as it would have in a round of live ammunition. Because the shells had propellant but nothing to propel, our parents thought they were harmless.

We collected the empty shells and used hammers to push them into cartridges, forming long strings of bullets. Those of us who were still little—I was seven—pretended to feed these into machine guns on days when we were Americans or Germans, or we wore them as bandoleers on days when we fought alongside Pancho Villa.

When we were lucky, we found shells with the red paper tips intact—meaning the shell was still filled with gunpowder. These we brought back to the munitions factory in our garage, where we used large nails to tap out the paper seal and poured the precious explosive into peanut butter jars. We'd get a teaspoon of powder from each red-dotted shell, and at times, our stash would reach a quart or more.

The collecting, storing, and trading of gunpowder was a fine hobby in its own right, one that could occupy a boy for days at a time. But the blowing up of things gave us the greatest joy.

We made intricate battlefield scenes, using tiny soldiers and bunkers built with popsicle sticks, and then blew them up. At this age, before the older kids entrusted me with the power of ignition, I was a builder, filling the scenes with the tiny details that made the destruction so terrible and inhumane. There was the row of kneeling soldiers who would be hit with shrapnel, and the doomed prone marksmen trapped in the ditch that would surely burn. I caked model airplanes and ships with gobs of glue so that a fire lingered after the explosion ignited by an older boy. I watched gopher holes, anthills, and piles of dried wood blown up, for an entire summer, it seemed.

I would learn, when it was my turn, to be exceedingly careful, meticulous even, in blowing things up. We lit long trails of gunpowder cautiously, striking the match away from us and touching just the very end of the gray line. We were smart enough to watch it sparkle only out of the corner of our eye while we ran for cover behind a section of cement pipe. No one was hurt in these games—at least not any humans.

The navy base closed eventually, and the gunfire faded. Our explosive fixes, for a time, came instead from sliced-open M-80s and firecrackers. It took much longer to fill a jar, and we never again had patience enough, or powder enough, to fill one. Even if we had, the powder from our new sources seemed too fine a grain, with a greasiness that stained both hands and jeans. I missed the heavier grain that poured out of shotgun shells without the faintest puff. Like Cream of Wheat or grilled cheese sandwiches, the gunpowder of my youth fits among the smells and textures of my best childhood memories.

Fifty-seven children lived in the two rows of houses facing each other on our one block of Cypress Avenue. When we added in the kids from Sycamore and Magnolia, we hit more than eighty. We were proud of our numbers, sensing great possibilities on our street. It seemed larger than life, not in hindsight but then, as it was happening. We were like the Russian army; our power was in the capacity to overwhelm, and we could overwhelm kids from other streets who might prefer to play by rules other than the ones we chose.

We played games on an epic scale, especially one called Tomahawk. Essentially hide-and-seek played with teams, insanely complicated details made our street's version both unique and renowned—or so we thought. Tomahawk games involved two teams, often with a dozen or more kids on each side. At seven, I was filler—an extra—added to give the game a more majestic feel, or to stop my whining. The playing field usually included the front and back yards of forty or more houses; in some games, even the interiors of a few houses were included. The game required teamwork and strategy, with occasional intrigue. Individual speed and cunning were highly valued, giving a distinct advantage to the Fanucchis, all of whom were fast. The chases could be brilliant. A bold dash across front lawns or into the street was a suicide mission but could free teammates already captured. Going up and over a series of fences allowed time enough for the pursuing team to get close, but there was always the prospect of a pursuer slipping or ripping a pair of jeans on a snag. We made our decisions in these games with the knowledge that the story to follow mattered as much as the act;

the mere possibility that a story might come of it made great risks worth taking.

The best stories, and the best chases, involved sprints atop fence posts. I was never directly involved in one—certainly not at this age—but I clung to the breathtaking sight of Chris Ranney chasing Jimmy Molesky at what looked to be full speed, each boy racing along the redwood two-by-fours that provided the upper framing of six-foot-tall fences. Boys racing on fence tops like Jesus walking on water. It was a moment of epiphany: We lived in a great place.

The houses on Cypress Avenue were always open, or so it seemed. No one locked their doors, and we could come and go as we pleased. It was all one block on the outside, an amorphous mix of parents, kids, toys, and tools. Inside the houses, though, the differences seemed exotic, particularly the differences in food and smells. Some of the mothers took hours to cook a sauce— unheard of in our family—and their homes smelled magical all day long. In some houses, the odor of garlic was overpowering, making them intolerable hiding places during Tomahawk. A few were meticulously neat, though we rarely made it through the doorway on those. And there were the homes in which grandparents lived with the family or visited often; this meant we had to be quiet, but also meant the parents needed to show restraint when yelling.

Despite the openness, there could be privacy for those who

demanded it. Some houses and yards we avoided. Ski and Eva's house was one of them—we didn't knock on their door and we avoided their yard. They were the only grown-ups we addressed by their first names, but they still appeared more distant than the others. They were urbane, the only childless couple on the street, and may have taken a game that involved the use of their property as an insult to them personally, when in fact our presence in their back shed was just a consequence of living near children. Mr. Mailhoit methodically pounded two-inch nails in a neat row along the top of their fence. He left half of each nail exposed above the redwood, then went back with wire cutters and cut off the nail heads, leaving a row of sharp points. It wasn't impossible to hop his fence, but it was inconvenient, so we gave him room. Pulled drapes in the morning meant a family wasn't yet up; pulled drapes in the afternoon said it wasn't a good time to knock. A strange car in front of the Bart's house—Mrs. Bart, who drove a Thunderbird and was the only divorcee we knew— was not to be mentioned. Mrs. Reynolds was nervous if kids jumped her fence, so we gave her distance.

Some invasions were unavoidable, partly because the neighborhood considered its children community property. When I was seven, the Flick twins, Pam and Sheila, attended their junior prom. While they prepared to leave, more than thirty kids lined the sidewalk in front of their house. As the glamorous twins emerged with their dates, corsages and boutonnieres freshly in place, we let go with a chorus of "ooooo" and "aaahhh." It turned into applause, proof of our genuine pleasure at seeing two of our own look so splendid. Thus began a tradition that would last, in one form or another, for more than fifteen years. Aileen and Terry endured it, or reveled in it—I don't really know which—and one neighbor worked to build an audience for one of Anne's prom departures, as our street was no longer filled with young kids by then. When Kathy's prom came, she was disappointed to see no children on the sidewalk for her walk down our front steps. But her heart leaped when she and her date turned the corner onto Sycamore, and they heard the giant blast of a fire truck's horn. Our brother, Pat, by then a San Bruno firefighter, escorted her out of town, red lights flashing all the way.

A few bullies lived on our street, but they never had much power; the parents may not have noticed the gunpowder, but they watched us closely enough to know if we were treating each other well. Kids were ditched occasionally, some much more than others, but that couldn't be helped: Kids had a right to choose their friends, so long as they didn't pick on those who weren't quite in favor.

There were problems in all the houses on Cypress Avenue. Some were the standard fare of family woes; some were not. There was sadness, at our house and at others. There were fathers who drank and families that repressed. There were moms who drank, at the time almost unthinkable. There were girls who got pregnant and there were boys who caused the same heartbreak, the same confused emotions, in other families. There was worse, I'm sure.

But the street was elixir. The symptoms of whatever problems lay behind the doors on Cypress were in remission when we hit the pavement, flooding the neighborhood with our ambitions for the day. One day, we might fan out to inspect the empty buildings at the navy base, using a set of calls to signal the all-clear. On another, we might have a festival in the backyard, pooling our money to invest in prizes good enough to lure cash from kids on other streets. If you wanted company, you could always find someone, a kid or a parent, who had time. It was a cacophony, and there was beauty and solace—even cover—in all of that noise.

In a house with six children, being the one to collect the mail was a treat.

During the summer or on weekends, if I was home late in the morning, I might notice dogs barking in a progression up the street, a sign that the mailman would soon be coming up and over our hill. If it was quiet in our house, I might hear the faint sounds of mailboxes opening and closing. At this point, if other kids were home, I positioned myself close to the kitchen door. There, I could hear the mailman pushing letters through the narrow slot on the wall of our garage. The opening had a copper cover, which closed heavily as he pulled his hand away; it bounced against the stucco, with a loud "chink!" It was the sound of a metal grenade landing on concrete, awaiting detonation. This is when the others would notice, but I would already be in the garage, pouncing on the incoming charge.

For a few moments, I had information no one else in our family could have. It was a power I loved. I skimmed the letters and the mix of bills—by the second grade, I knew which were predictable and which were troubling. I knew, before anyone else, if moods would change. On the best days, a postcard would arrive from a traveling aunt, cousin, or friend. These were fair game for any and all to read. Nearly all the postcards we ever received went into a shoebox in the hall closet, and on rainy days we took world tours, with a heavy emphasis on Disneyland, San Diego, and the other California spots our friends had been able to visit.

During the last day or two of the month, fetching the mail was important. Two big green checks were scheduled to arrive on the last day and did so more often than not. One, from the Social Security Administration, was for an amount based on the contributions deducted from my father's salary over the years. The other, from the Veterans' Administration, was a set amount for the young survivors of anyone with military service. The sources of these funds were important to my mother. The Social Security checks did not mean we were on the dole, she reminded us; our father had paid into the fund and we were simply being paid back. The Veterans' checks were a gift from a grateful nation, yet another benefit—besides our freedom—of our father's military service. If the checks had arrived—those with the words *United States of America, Department of the Treasury* written in formal government script—Mom took us younger kids instantly to the bank and to the Lucky Supermarket. We received no treats or special candy on these trips, but the experience felt treat-like—we had counted on something and it had happened. If the checks had not arrived, I would bear the news, my task not unlike the poor corporal forced to deliver telegrams that began, "With deepest sympathy, and the gratitude of a nation, I regret to inform you. . . ." Mom's response was stoic; she genuinely tried to hide her frustration. She would wait a respectable time, half an hour or more, before going to her room, closing the door, and crying. By the end of the month, our money had run out; the nation, however grateful, could not sustain us for the next day or two.

Mom segregated funds as soon as they became available. Ten dollars a month in the bank's Christmas Club meant there would be $120 at the end of the year—$20 per kid for presents. Another ten dollars each month was set for a summer vacation; the cabin was $70, leaving extra cash for gasoline and for Mom to spring for rounds of fries or ice cream. Money was set aside for school uniforms, to be purchased every August. The trick was to avoid any unpredictable expenses, to flatten out the curve of spending. A spike in the electric bill of one or two dollars was noticeable. It was rare for there to be more than three lights on in our house at once, and leaving a room empty with the light on was committing the sin of squander. It wasn't an unforgivable sin—no such sins existed, to our knowledge—but it was a hard one to forget. Car repairs were always devastating.

We bought clothes once a year, and only replaced ones we had grown out of or had worn through. Jeans and T-shirts were hard to make on the family sewing machine—denim would break the needle—and my brother was seven years older than me, so I was one who always got new clothes. I never once as a child wore hand-me-downs, a privilege I was acutely aware of but never discussed. My sisters usually wore dresses and blouses made by our mother—or by themselves as they got older and learned to sew. These would be passed from the oldest girl to the youngest. In the Christmas photo from when I was seven, all four Sweeney girls are wearing similar dresses made of the same fabric. It was easy for my mom, and on that day it looked cute. But it also meant that the youngest, Kathy, could wear what looked to be the same dress for eight years or more. Shoes were a challenge, as Mom had to balance issues of quality and price with the knowledge that I would likely grow out of them in half a year. She applied the notion of planned obsolescence as best she could: A shoe should wear out the same week it became too small. If it lasted longer, we were wasting money.

When I was in second grade, our great aunt Grace took the entire family to dinner at the New Southern, a restaurant three miles from our house. It was the first time in my life that I ordered dinner from a menu and sat back as a waiter brought food to my table. It never occurred to me that some families dined out often; it never occurred to me that this might be a reason to be jealous. That meal with Aunt Grace was a big event, one we talked about for years. My second dinner in a restaurant would not be for nine more years, the night of my junior prom. Aileen, also unfamiliar with restaurants, caused a minor family scandal when she ordered Jell-O for dinner before attending the Soph-Hop with Brian Kelly, Chick and Dolores Kelly's son. Too nervous to eat, Aileen thought Jell-O looked like the only thing she could keep down. My mother was appalled the next day and tried to point out that it might have been better, perhaps more refined, to instead pick at a salad or spoon some soup. My sister didn't know better, none of us did. We had never been refined.

There always seemed to be enough food in our house. We ate the cheap stuff, and we ate it often. If the big green checks were stuck in the mail, we ate macaroni and cheese every night until the money came in. As a young boy, I loved the taste and the texture, even the garish yellow-orange color. Later, when our finances became marginally more secure, Mom never served it again, a break I wasn't aware of until I was off at college. Early in my freshman year, the dorm served macaroni and cheese, and I grabbed a plateful. I didn't notice a thing about it, but after just a few bites, I was unable to push away from the table quickly enough. I vomited right there, covering my tray, and have avoided the stuff ever since. My brother Pat has not eaten it either, not for thirty years.

On Sundays, we occasionally stopped at the Roma Delicatessen on the way home from church, where Mom would purchase fifty cents worth of salami. At the time, I suspect it was a quarter pound or more, but the overall weight was not what mattered to us: Each of us kids would get two pieces of salami. And so, starting at eleven o'clock on Sunday mornings, we had something to look forward to: two pieces of salami. Some days, I cut my allotment of two into many smaller pieces, placing each on top of its own saltine cracker. Other days I loaded up everything I had—all two pieces—on a bed of crackers, creating one glorious sandwich that was gone in two bites. I might eat my share right away; I might hold off until later in the day. It was brilliant work on our mom's part, that she could help us find satisfaction in such a small serving.

Our mother loved good, red meat, and occasionally she craved it. She would rather go two weeks without hamburgers or chicken so we could have roast beef just once that month. We heard about these desires often, but rarely saw them satisfied. I sometimes suspect that all of her resentments—all of her frustrations, jealousies, and heartaches—became focused on this one sensual delight. If that's true, it fit a pattern in our house: not to complain about the real deal, but about something else. It may have seemed more reasonable to complain about meat than about the fact that she was tired and alone in a crowded house, with no prospects for change. For her thirty-fifth birthday, my brother used some of his paper route profits to give Mom a T-bone steak as a present. I don't remember the actual steak, but as a young boy, I heard Mom say several times over that it was the best present she would ever receive. It was proof to her that her son, a ten-year-old boy, understood her plight. I don't know if my brother understood all of that. I don't know if he was trying to improve her lot for that one moment, or quietly admitting that he could not.

On the morning of my seventh birthday, I ate two fried eggs. It was the one day each year when we were entitled to two eggs, and it was as special, almost, as opening presents. Birthday dinners depended on where we stood financially. Terry, whose birthday fell on the second of the month, had a better chance of choosing her meal than I did, with my birthday falling on the twenty-ninth. Anne's birthday, falling in December, was never well timed.

If the meals were lackluster, how we ate was impressive. Molly Bart, a neighbor who was Terry's age, stayed over at our house one night when her mother was on a date. I noticed nothing unusual about the occasion, except that we may have been allowed to stay up later than normal. But the next weekend, when her mother was out again, Molly brought her own box of cereal and her own small carton of milk. She ate slowly and calmly, while the rest of us ate as we always did—quickly and voraciously. The contrast made for a pathetic sight, and for at least a few minutes, I suspect we felt chastened by the notion that if someone unused to our eating habits didn't act quickly, they would barely get food. But that emotion shifted into a source of pride. Be quick or be hungry, either way was fine with us.

Amid all of this, twenty bucks a month went to St. Robert's Church. Every week, Mom subtly placed a fiver in the envelope and dropped it in the collection basket. She never raised the topic of tithing with us, but I occasionally asked how much she gave, mostly because I found it stunning and wanted to hear her say it out loud. I was proud of her, though I never thought to say so. My mom was getting beaten up financially—something big was always breaking—but there appeared to be nothing that could knock her out. If there was bad news in the middle of the week, she brushed herself off and smiled as she dropped the envelope in the basket. It was impressive.

As the offertory hymn was sung during mass, I listened to the sounds of the basket being passed. I grew to dislike the sound I was listening for intently, the sound of tumbling coins. My mom was dropping in paper, real money, and some of those coins were falling from the hands of dads or from families that I knew had money. Pocket change was all they had for the priests. Shame on them, I thought, and I slipped into anger and resentment just before the Gloria and the Consecration itself.

Jealousy seemed petty to me, or perhaps it was labeled as petty by our mom and by the priests, so I couldn't allow myself to feel jealous for those kids whose families had more money than mine. And jealousy was linked in obvious ways to sadness, which we knew was a room we were not to enter. I settled in to a comfortable anger. When I could justify it with righteousness—these people weren't giving the church its due—it felt perfect and natural. I wasn't petty, I thought; I was right. I was angry and I was right.

There were more times, though, when I lacked the certainty and slipped into confusion or numbness.

When I was eight, men from the St. Vincent de Paul Society visited our house twice. Just as they had done in previous years, they dropped by on the night before Thanksgiving and two days before Christmas. These were the men who stood quietly at the church doors once a month, taking up a special collection for the poor. Theirs was not the usual passing of the hat, which was a bustle of activity amid the music of the Ordinary. The gifts collected by the St. Vincent de Paul men were clearly for the poor, for the forlorn, for those barely touched by God's mercy. These were gifts not of piety but of pity. And, it turns out, they were for us.

The men—I can remember Mr. Wargo and Mr. Waskowiak, but not the others—crowded into our foyer on a November night, progressing no further. There, they handed over a huge turkey and sacks full of cans, boxes, and bags that contained the fixings and trimmings of a holiday feast. They said very little, not wanting to call attention to something that their very visit had called attention to. We knew in advance that they were coming—one had called to tell Mom she needn't shop—and we were to be polite and grateful in their presence, something that was not hard for me to be in those moments. I was thrilled by their presence. I loved turkey, but I loved these men more than anything. I loved their goodness, their service. It was breathtaking, really, and I was enthralled. Men treating my mother and us kids with generosity, with concern, with kindness. I loved that they would do this for us and for others. I wanted to be like them. I wanted to be them. I would always give to them when I had money of my own, I told myself.

When the men had said their good-byes, Mom closed the

door gently, taking care not to slam it. In the kitchen, she sorted through the bags, taking out those things she knew her children would not eat—yams, exotic olives, antipasto, and all the items that other families thought of as treats. Then there were the items that we would eat but that she could have bought or made for far less money. She started to sigh as she put things away in the cupboards.

"These pie crusts cost ninety cents," she said. "I could have made one for pennies." Her resentment built with each item pulled from the bag.

"Why didn't they just give money? Why do they waste money on these things? You kids will never eat this stuff."

Her tears started now but didn't interrupt the flow, didn't interrupt the building hurt or anger or whatever it was that she was feeling.

"Why did they buy brand names? Why do we need four cans of pumpkin pie filling when no one here will eat it?"

Now the tears could not stop and came with such force that she could no longer speak. She tried to apologize to us for saying things about these men who had been so helpful. But she couldn't, no matter how hard she tried. Her tears were both angry and sad, and even if she could have spoken aloud at this point, she could not really have apologized. Anne, always Mom's greatest defender, tried to hover over her, tried to help her see that it was okay to be angry. Mom raced past us and into her room, slamming the door in a way that she rarely did. We stood hushed outside her door—Anne, Kathy, and I—listening to sobs cascading down from a woman's half-empty bed, waiting for a flood of tears to rush under the doorway.

It was so confusing, so utterly confusing. I had been so grateful only minutes earlier, so inspired, so happy. Only a year after learning the facts about Santa—that's how little I was—I was learning other hard lessons. I knew that my mother had been shamed, or, at the very least, I thought I had learned that the giving and accepting of gifts was complicated. I couldn't see then that it was even more complex, that my mother may have felt more than shame. It was the holidays, and she was alone with a houseful of children. Perhaps, for her, too, anger was easier than sadness. I couldn't see this then, not for her, not for myself.

Mom's bout did not last long. The next day was a holiday and our mother never, ever, let anything ruin the mood of a holiday. Not the death of our father, not the absence of money, not three kids with the measles, not the worst rainstorm any of us had ever seen—she recovered in time. Still, there were holidays when it felt as if we had all just been mugged, and this was one of them.

It was a holiday when I could sense I was missing something.

5

Watching Over Me

The summer of 1966 was a summer of noise.

Massive construction crews were razing the open lands at the navy base, where military operations had been scaled back and excess lands were sold off for private development. Rises were flattened and gullies were filled in. Oaks and older eucalyptus trees were spared, but the other varieties, and all of the bushes and grasses, were taken out. I could no longer find the springs that a friend and I had fallen into while hunting for salamanders. The site of one of my many baptisms, it was where the thrill of a good calamity was first revealed. The snapping cottonwood branch led the two of us, ultimately, to the base commander's office—he was my friend's father—where a handful of decorated officers roared with laughter and traded stories with us for what seemed like hours. The spring's creek had been diverted into an underground pipe, and other geographic touchstones were obliterated as well. The razing went so fast that we never had time for a last gunpowder run.

The heartbreak associated with the loss of open lands was

obscured, at least in our case, because construction noises were also coming from our own backyard. Our father's insurance settlement, after paying off debts acquired when he was still alive, would pay for an addition to our house. A little more than four years after his death, we added a bedroom, family room, and second bathroom.

The contractor was Mr. Waskowiak, a St. Robert's parishioner and one of the St. Vincent de Paul men. He let me bang hammers to stay busy, and he taught me how to use a miter saw. There was real work for the family as well, though, and all of the kids were to help. With Uncle Roger leading the way, we painted the house, inside and out. Early in my third-grade year, I spent several weekends scraping, sanding, and priming. Uncle Roger raced around the house with his rollers, covering the stucco with fresh paint almost as fast as we could move the heavy drop cloths. Pat and Aileen were old enough and steady enough to do finish work, so they did much of the trim.

With the addition, we had hit the lottery. Overnight, we went from three kids a room down to two. Pat and I moved to the new bedroom in the back of the house. Boys only from now on, and we lined our new shelves with liquor displays that he got from his job at Zanetti's Liquor Store. Twin beds, a dresser, and there was room, even, for a desk. I had my own half of the closet. With Pat in high school and working at least one job now, the room was mostly mine. I had privacy, a place to change my clothes without asking a girl to leave the room. It was away from everything else, this new room, and Mom needed to walk through the dining room, family room, and a short hallway just to get to me. Our room shared a common wall with Mom's room, and she banged a hand on the wall if I was needed. Mostly, she hit the wall on Wednesday mornings, when the garbage trucks made their noise and I had inevitably forgotten to take out the trash the night before.

The summer's noise cleared a path for genuine silence.

I now had a place to go, a place to think. At night, I often fell asleep while listening to Giants games on the radio, but in the off-season, or if they played on the East Coast and the game ended early in our time zone, I would lie in silence, away from the family. I had long conversations with myself, moving my lips as I talked, mostly imagining my life in the future, but also trying to piece together things that had already happened. Sometimes I thought of Daddy. I remember nights when I wondered what his corpse might look like after all those years. It was a gruesome thought, and it seems now, in hindsight, like a means of holding onto a family habit of avoiding him.

Had I been introspective before we added on, I might never have known it. The cacophony and distractions served a purpose—our lives were full of fun and stimulus—but they also kept me from exploring what was missing, in my family and in myself. Looking back, I don't fully understand what was cause and what was effect. I don't know if I began to more clearly notice what was missing in my life because of the silence or if, after five years, what was missing could no longer be ignored.

Our father was buried in the Golden Gate National Cemetery, a little more than a mile from our house, just on the other side of the construction site that was once the navy base. Each grave is marked by a white marble stone, two feet high and rounded at the top. From a distance, they are all exactly the same—more than a hundred thousand markers fanning out across a slight incline. It is neat as can be, the rows perfectly placed, the lawn cut as close to the stones as an industrial mower will allow. A few scattered trees are the only breaks. The entry is through massive ornate gates, not quite pearly but full of polished brass and wrought iron.

Even five years after Daddy's death, I visited the cemetery fairly often, mostly with Grandma and Grandpa Sweeney. If the weather was bad or if we were hurrying on the way to their house, we said a full decade of the rosary—the sorrowful decade—as we drove by. On most trips, though, we stopped to visit and say our rosary in the presence of his grave. We brought flowers—from Grandma's backyard or from ours—wrapped in foil and soaking in a jar full of water. After one of us kids poured the water into the can set into the lawn in front of his grave and placed the flowers neatly, Grandma leaned down on her one good knee to rearrange them and pull furiously at any weeds or tall grass standing against the stone. Her lips quivered as she did this, just as they nearly always quivered when we were in or near the cemetery. Some days we knelt, some days we stood, and on most days the dominant sound was of the wind blowing through the graveyard on its way down the hill and out across the San Francisco Bay.

I marveled over the symmetry of a national cemetery. The graves were perfectly aligned, with each headstone fitting neatly into four straight lines: north to south, east to west, and the two diagonals, northeast to southwest, and southeast to northwest. The rows flowed uninterrupted by knolls or declines in the grass. I stood next to a grave near my daddy's, and slowly turned around, hoping to give the impression that I was taking in the massive loss of humanity that stretched before me. But really I was counting the number of straight lines, eight, that flowed from each grave. I loved seeing the clutter of white stones snap into focus, into one of the eight straight lines, as I spun slowly in my circle. Each grave as the center of a wheel, as the center of a universe. Sometimes I strolled the grounds, looking for admirals, generals, or someone whose birth date might have meaning in our family. Some days I strolled a great distance before returning to my grandparents, who stood quizzically at the grave.

There were times when it was a beautiful setting. On Memorial Day each year, small American flags were methodically placed in front of each headstone, an elegant gesture of remembrance, loyalty, or patriotism. We always visited Daddy's grave when the flags were out, and it would lead to a good week. Our mom, with a weakness for symbolism, looked both proud and peaceful as she drove away from the graveyard, the mood sticking with her and with us. Grandpa Sweeney talked of those who had placed the flags. "The Boy Scouts," he would say. "They always remember." I knew then as I held his hand that I too would always remember, though I wasn't quite sure what it would be, or who it would be, that I remembered.

I touched Daddy's marker always on these visits, quietly resting my palm atop the stone. Sometimes I traced my index finger through the engraved letters of his name, hoping to feel something, something besides the weathered marble. This part of the visit was obligatory—I just had to touch that stone—but always disappointing. I could feel no connection. He was dead and buried and that was that. I couldn't call up feelings of sadness simply from proximity to his remains, and my lack of sadness troubled me. What I did feel was the peace of open space, the quiet of an immense mowed lawn, and the chance to be reflective about the world and my circumstances. I appreciated the respectful tone of our visits, and the deference we would show to any other visitors who happened by on the way to their own sorrow or emptiness or both. I liked feeling the wind against my skin.

I really loved going to the cemetery. I just didn't feel what I thought I was supposed to feel there.

The particular form of Catholicism in which I was raised taught that good might come from suffering. This was not a statement about training or toughening, as if to suggest that suffering through a ten-mile run might make me stronger, or that suffering through impoverishment might make me more resilient.

This was about goodness. It was about good coming from something that appeared to be bad. It was a way to turn suffering into heroism.

Jesus had died on the cross not for his salvation, but ours. On a daily basis, and without giving up our life, we could do the same for others. This was not for temporal gain or to merely save a life. No, we could save souls. I believed this then, wholly. The nuns and priests often explained the notion of "offering it up," of bearing the suffering with a purpose. We were to consciously and quietly endure our own sorrow, our own disappointment, our own suffering and pain, in the name of someone who had gone before us into death. If they were not yet in heaven, our offerings might get them closer. The need was endless. All the children in limbo. All those lost ones in purgatory who were long dead and forgotten. All the souls waiting for salvation. Some of them fathers. One of them, perhaps, mine.

Five years after his death, I rarely thought of Daddy, of the Jim Sweeney who had walked the earth. But when I did think of him, it was most often as a soul I needed to save, as a lost corpse whose salvation depended on me. He was my father and I was only eight, but I was responsible for him. My acts of heroism on his behalf—when I would offer things up for him—were tiny. On occasions when I felt sad, I acted cheerfully. I sat patiently with Grandma when I wanted to leave. I did the dishes when it wasn't my night. These were all rare occasions, but their rarity was not cause to celebrate when I finally did offer something up. They were instead a reminder to me that he was floating in the ethers and I wasn't doing enough to help him. All of this I held within me. Offering it up required silence and stoicism. To talk about it would have made it not about him, but about me. It would deny the very intent.

I could also feel, most likely having absorbed it from books and movies, that my dead father was watching over me. In films, the image was meant as support, as if the dead father still offered a loving shoulder on which the film's protagonist could lean. Or it was intended to be congratulatory, as if the dead father might be looking on with pride. But for me, the notion of a constant observer—particularly if the observer was one whose soul might depend on my good works—was a harrowing one. If he could watch over me, if he could see me at all times, he could see my failures. He could see all those times when I broke rules or didn't act with pure motives. If he could be proud, he could also feel shame, an awareness that magnified my moments of personal disappointment.

By this point, though responsible for my father, I could not remember him. Occasional strangers would say to me, "Your dad was a great guy," but they never offered more details. And I knew the stories of the days surrounding his death. But these were not my memories; they were stories told to me by others. I had a vague recollection of sitting on his lap, at the wheel of a parked street sweeper in the city maintenance yard, his hairy arms wrapping round me. No words, facial expression, or movements. Just the sense of touch, the feel of Daddy's arms wrapped around mine. Back then, the memory didn't seem like much, and the opaqueness made me wonder how real it was, anyway.

I no longer had anything that was my father. Though I was aware that at times I missed having a father—mostly for the money I thought a dad would bring in—I was also aware that I did not miss him. Not Jim Sweeney. I didn't know him.

While I did not miss my father, I still felt I was missing something. I felt incomplete, and I was afraid that I might always be incomplete.

6

Father Figures

At the age of eight, I began to worry about what I might lack as someone who grew up without a dad. I wondered whether I could ever be a good father if I didn't have a father of my own. In those hazy minutes between bedtime and sleep, I lingered over the fact that I would not have the classic point of reference—my old man—at crucial points in my life. I thought of the presumed moments of crisis—as a father and as a man—when grown men say to themselves, "My old man would have done it this way." How could I know what to do or say if I had never seen it done, if I had never been in the room? How could I be a good father?

My ambitions then did not focus on family or parenthood; I didn't see fatherhood as my highest calling. I would have a career unlike any in my family and would do great things—of that, I was certain. But, still, I was missing something. I would not be complete. Worse, I might fail at something that mattered. I might fail at being a good father. I might fail at being a good man.

And so I developed a plan.

Sitting on the floor of my new room and leaning against the back of my twin bed, I wrote my first-ever journal entry in a composition notebook I had recently been given. In slow cursive, I described my plan for learning how to be a good father.

I would pick out three men, and they would teach me how. I would not tell them—they could not know of their role or that they were being observed—but I would watch them closely, carefully, studying them as fathers. I would take every opportunity to sit by them, listen to them, learn from them. They would be the ones I relied on for advice, the ones I would remember on that day in the future when I felt the need to say, "I remember when."

My scheme had a formality and simplicity that makes me wonder now about why I felt this need so clearly. It may have come from the image of television fathers, the perfect ones who sat on the edge of the bed and had the right words to close the week's episode. It may have come from Catholicism, with its emphasis on male leaders who stood before the crowd and spoke with insight and authority. It may have been that Pat was now rarely around, so often out with friends or working to save for college, or that my overnight visits to Grandma and Grandpa Sweeney's house were now infrequent; the men I had relied on were slipping away from me. Perhaps I did not understand my emptiness; perhaps I was finding a way to replace sadness with worry. I don't know what it was. I just recall the emptiness, and the feeling that I might somehow, and always, be incomplete.

I had two dads in mind right away: Jim Gaffney and Chick Kelly. Both of them were joined through marriage to Mom's St. Cecilia's clique and were obvious choices. By the time I finished writing on that afternoon, I had adopted them for life.

Jim Gaffney was Alice's husband and the father of their seven children, most of whom were matched in age with a Sweeney kid.

I didn't see Jim often, perhaps three or four times a year, but he was the most graceful dad I knew. DiMaggio with kids running around. Classically tall, dark, and handsome, with angular features, his hair was always neatly clipped. He wore knit slacks, shirts that fit closely, and cardigan sweaters that I thought were elegant. He fastened only the bottom two buttons on his cardigans, occasionally pushing up the sleeves. It was a style I copied on the wool sweater of my St. Robert's school uniform, causing my mom to constantly remind me that it was bad for the sleeves to push them up. He was the only grown-up I knew who lifted weights. In his garage, for a few minutes on most evenings, he pumped iron. I always took a quiet garage tour—given by one of his sons—to see the bars, weights, and clamps neatly aligned on the shelves. Jim Gaffney was lean, muscular, and strong. He cared about his appearance but seemed comfortable with his vanity, such as it was. He showed it was okay to be aware of one's own personal style.

The Gaffneys were wealthy. They had a huge spread in Atherton, a town of great mystery and importance to us because it was also the home, at the time, of Willie Mays. It was farther down the peninsula and much warmer than San Bruno. Most of the native oaks, it seemed, had survived the homebuilding period; streets wended their way around ancient trees, and thick limbs reached over and across the asphalt. The drive down Tuscaloosa Avenue felt like a visit to the country; walking through their house and into the yard felt like passage to an amusement park. They had an L-shaped pool, with a tetherball pole standing in the shallow waters, and both a diving board and slide in the deep end. The slide was ten feet high, with water running down it, and the drop from the top of the slide to the deep of the pool seemed instant. There was a separate building next to the pool—a cabana, they called it—where guests could change or relax or play pool, perhaps even stand around and drink sodas. They had a Ping-Pong table, lawn games, and enough chaise longues to deprive us of the chance to stake one out and argue over turf. Their house was clearly divided into two sections, something we had not really seen before. The living quarters were where noise was made and where us kids spent most of our time when visiting. The dining and entertaining areas were neater and calmer; it was where the adults could talk in quiet. There were no barriers—we could come and go if we pleased—but the rules were different in rooms where the adults talked. We could listen in, even join in, so long as we didn't interrupt.

I was aware of their wealth, just as I was aware then that I did not resent them for it. It was an awareness that became more important over the years, when my jealousies of the rich strayed toward contempt. In the case of Mr. Gaffney—the only name I ever used to address him—I knew his money had come from hard work. Sure there was luck: He was born into a family that owned something. But there was also the work.

He ran Gaffney Meats, a wholesale meatpacking firm his family owned for three generations. Usually up at four in the morning to be at the warehouse in San Francisco when animal carcasses were unloaded, he supervised the process, with gloved hands and a heavy coat. Later in the mornings, he made rounds to the butcher shops and restaurants that were the bulk of his clientele, where a Gaffney Meats hindquarter would become flank steaks, round steaks, and shanks. One client we knew of was Candlestick Park, where Giants fans ate hamburgers made with Gaffney Meats, as the small advertisement in the game day program made clear. That he worked hard was something we knew, partly because we saw it in his hands, partly because the mothers found a way to tell us this. Good fathers worked hard.

His children worked hard as well. Their lawn was immense, and the shrubs, bushes, and flowers were neatly placed, for esthetics and privacy. But the Gaffneys had no gardener. I knew little about professional gardeners, only that this was the kind of place where gardeners made their living. They would not make their living at the Gaffneys, though, because Mr. Gaffney considered yard work to be the kids' work. If the children were to benefit from the family's wealth, they would need to earn it. The Gaffney kids may have seemed rich to us, but they weren't rich kids: They had more chores and bigger chores than we did. I respected them for it. I respected him for it.

Not long after I chose him as mine, he told me that he admired my mother. We were standing alone in their kitchen, and he had just left a conversation with his wife, Alice, and my mother. I felt something stirring in me as he said this, and I sensed that the conversation had weight for him, too. It may have been that he was sentimental, prone to tears when he felt something deeply, and was speaking deliberately to stop a rush. Perhaps I could tell he was choosing to say something important to me. It may also have been his choice of the word *admire,* which at the time seemed to me to be a term used more often for males, for heroes. It was different from saying that she was a good mom, that she was doing a fine job raising kids on her own, that she was pretty or fun or sweet. Those things could be expected; they were, after all, what I had come to expect in my mother. But Mr. Gaffney, a father I had chosen, was saying something very different. He admired my mother. I don't remember the exact context, how it came up in the conversation we were having, but I'm certain he was saying something he wanted me to know, something he wanted me to understand. At eight, it felt man-to-man. And I thought it interesting that this father admired my mother, that a good father would admire a woman.

Chick Kelly was Dolores's husband, father to their nine children. He grew up in the same San Francisco neighborhood and parish as Dolores, Marian, and the other St. Cecilia's girls, but he went to different schools than they did, so their paths rarely crossed. In high school, though, the crossing wasn't necessary for Chick to be noticed. He was a star, an All-City football player as a tackle, a position that required both strength and speed, especially back then when they played in tiny leather helmets. It didn't hurt to be huge either, and Chick was. All of this was many years before I was born, and something I never heard him discuss, but it was still part of his lore, at least the lore our mother explained to us. It may have been a way of explaining his size and presence; he was big enough to be intimidating. It may have been a way to explain his charisma; he was not loud, but he filled a room, as if it was expected of him from a very young age. It may simply have been a handle, a way to show he was special, because we all sensed that he was, and the real reasons were more subtle, less obvious.

He was a butcher, a foreman at the John Morrel meatpacking plant across the bay in Oakland. He, too, worked long hours—he had little choice in supporting nine children—and the hours were early ones. Out of the house by four most mornings, he could work twelve hours and still be home by five in the evening. We knew all this because a nighttime visit to the Kellys wound down early; bedtime on a weeknight was nine. Weekends were different, because everyone stayed up late; Chick did and the kids did, and Chick would sleep as long as he wanted on Saturdays. If we stopped by at noon, he would still be asleep.

He worked on, and supervised, an assembly line to process meat. Giant carcasses of beef, pork, and lamb slid through the chilled plant on steel hooks, and the beasts were pared down to edible portions along the way. His entire day was spent in ice-cold rooms and lockers, so he wore heavy boots with double socks, several shirts, and more than one coat. I assume the work is what kept him strong. The warm sting of his handshake left my hand tingling for whole minutes.

The Kellys lived ten miles from us, but we saw them often. In the summertime, the moms loaded up most or all of the kids and headed to San Mateo Park for an occasional picnic.

If we were visiting in the evening, we usually arrived after dinner, but if only a subset of Sweeneys was visiting, we might come for a meal. Every family said grace back then, at least every family we knew, and eating didn't commence until the amen was uttered. At the Kellys, Chick added a requirement: No one touched their food until grace was said and until Dolores was seated at the table. For Chick, it was important to say it aloud.

"Don't even *think* about eating until your mother is seated and comfortable" is how he put it. Jesus and your mother—ignore either and Chick's wrath might be greater than God's.

The shortest dinner at the Kellys might last an hour, and a Saturday night dinner might last two. Their table was a four-foot-by-eight-foot sheet of plywood laid flat upon a smaller table, and the lazy Susan, filled with condiments and paper napkins, spun constantly, kids reaching in from all angles. Everyone spoke, and though there were often many conversations going at once, Chick and Dolores managed to orchestrate it. At our house, after thirty minutes the kids would leave the conversation to the adults, but not here. Everyone chimed in. I loved it. It was a chance to join in with the older kids, and a chance to show off for adults. When friends were over, the Kelly kids seemed to revel in the length of their meals and the complexity of their conversations; they knew that no one else's dinners—no one's—were quite like this. Visitors were always called on by the parents, drawn into the conversation, but there was enough background noise at the ends of the table that no one felt on the spot.

Our family visits to their house were cacophonous. Fifteen kids would fan out among the clutter of bedrooms, constantly moving up and down the stairs. The TV remained on to entertain the two younger Kellys, who weren't matched in age by a Sweeney. Whichever Kelly washed the endless pile of dishes that night could play his or her choice of music on the kitchen radio, and did so loudly. Kelly kids were prone to shouting their pleasure or dissatisfaction, and the boys, who were growing to be their father's size, had booming voices. Amid all the noise, the three parents—Chick, Dolores, and my mom—would sit quietly in the living room to have their talk.

At some point on every visit, Chick stopped me to ask how I was. He stopped me with a look, opening his eyes wide and staring directly and closely into mine, as if to suggest that I should stop running just now because he wanted my attention. Or he stopped me by grabbing my arm as I shot past, holding it long enough, after the first question and answer, to show that I should relax because we were about to talk. He held my arm until he knew that my temporary angle of repose was right there, standing or sitting in front of him, engaged in a conversation with a man who had been a dear friend of Daddy's.

"Tell me what you're up to," he said, and did so in a tone that suggested he really wanted to know, that I could take my time in telling him if I wanted to. I told him about my accomplishments, and the work that may have led up to them. I talked about my ambitions. And I loved telling him funny stories, particularly those with a hint of irony. In hindsight, it seems as if there was something in the irony—the unspoken or indirect element—that made it feel to me as if we were saying more, and communicating about more, than what was on the surface. They weren't really conversations, then, because Chick mostly listened. He smiled big, with his mouth closed while I spoke, and sometimes he put his hand on my shoulder. He looked me in the eye longer than anyone.

He could get very, very mad. I never saw his anger, but I heard about it. Though the episodes were rare, his kids turned each one into a lasting story. Too much gin and he chased his brother-in-law on the beach in such a way that the kids were grateful their uncle was faster than their dad. That was it for the gin—that was the lesson they all drew. Tim broke a window and didn't 'fess up, and Dad let him have it. The stories were enough so that when Chick called up the stairs to tell us to keep it down, we did. We weren't afraid; we simply knew it was a good idea. The contrast with our house, without a loud or dominant male voice, was dramatic. Anger was not tolerated by our mom—a burst on my part would be demeaned with an understated, "Temper! Temper!" The remark would of course make me angrier. But for the Kellys it was part of their lore, part of life. His anger was accepted, respected even.

At the time I adopted him, he had just recently made one of his regular visits to our house, stopping by after work, bringing a massive package of fresh meat wrapped in white butcher paper. The kitchen counter was covered that day with flank steaks, ground beef, and pork chops. And there was a roast. By this point, he had stopped making excuses for the meat—in the past he might have mumbled that it had been cut wrong and would have been tossed otherwise—because we knew in our family that a meatpacker wasted nothing. He talked briefly to me and to each of the kids, then he and our mom sent us elsewhere. They sat closely at the dining room table, drinking black coffee. He sat still before her, looking at her and listening for a long, long time. These were the days—the only days—when we would not eat at exactly 5:15. Their conversation would not work by the clock but would end when it ended. Dinner would come later. I loved watching him talk with my mom. It was my mom sitting quietly with a man, looking directly at him and speaking to him only. There was no flirtation or anything that I might later come to know as sexual tension, but it was clearly different. My mom spoke in a different way when she spoke quietly to Chick. I thought my mom was beautiful then—prettier than any mom on the street—but she looked even better when she talked quietly to a man as strong as Chick. They were good friends, each deriving joy from the other, so his visits were not corporal works of mercy. Still, I liked that he came to check in on his friend, on my mom.

I watched these dads as closely as I said I would. When our families were together, I loitered in the living room with the grownups, watching the fathers go about their business. I watched the dads in the park with their kids, and in the stands when our school, St. Robert's, played against St. Timothy's or St. Pius. I watched the fathers watching their sons. I watched them shake hands, hug, and kiss. I watched them be husbands, watched how they treated their wives, and how they treated my mother. I sought them out to ask them questions, tell them my jokes, talk about stuff, anything. Never in a way that would reveal they were special—I couldn't bear to tell them how great the stakes were. Their words would break through the cacophony of a graduation party or a wedding and I would listen carefully: These were the words of a good father, I would think, a father I had chosen.

I now had two of my dads. One, Jim Gaffney, was elegant in reigning over a fairly reserved and refined family. The other,

Chick Kelly, rode herd on a boisterous bunch. I was in no hurry to find the third dad, though I knew I wanted three. This was not about convenience, it was about choice. If I was in a position to choose my dads, and I now was, I would choose the right ones. It would take me three years to find the third dad.

7

Ben Lomond

There were simple rules in our house.

Not wasting things was foremost—you finished your meal, turned off the lights, used both sides of paper, reused bags and foil, turned book pages carefully, folded sweaters when you removed them, used bathwater for more than one quick bath and never filled the tub more than three inches, turned off the water while brushing your teeth, saved coupons from newspapers and box tops, bought the store's brand rather than the one that advertised, and didn't leave tools out at night. Our home legal system was uncomplicated, but thorough. We followed the laws often and broke them often; when we broke them, we usually were aware of it.

By this time—I was in fourth grade now and we had three teenagers at home—there were rules I clearly saw as Mom's struggle not to lose control. We were not to receive phone calls during dinner. If it happened once, we told the friend it was a bad time to call; if it happened twice, we were fined a quarter. All phone calls were limited to ten minutes, which gave everyone access to the phone and also made it possible to reasonably share an outgoing line with another family. We still had a "party line," which allowed two families to save money by sharing a phone line; if you picked up the phone and heard other voices, you had to hang up and wait before making the call. Most party lines were shared by strangers, but we shared ours with the next door neighbors. If we hogged the line, they would know, and we'd have to face them, knowing what they knew. Or if they picked up the phone at an inopportune time, well, who knew what they might hear.

Gossip was not allowed. None of it. The standard cliché was used often in our house, as it was by the Gaffneys and Kellys and countless others: *If you can't say anything nice, don't say anything at all.* The Kellys, in fact, had a simple wooden plaque in their dining room, which Chick pointed to often: *Never criticize a man until you've walked a mile in his shoes.* The behavior was modeled by our mom and her entire circle of friends. I don't recall any of the grown-ups saying an unkind thing about another person. They criticized, but kept it to short and known truths, never wandering into conjecture. This ban on gossip segued into a hazier field, that of complaining, which occasionally sounded like gossip. Complaining was tolerated only below a certain level; the crossing point wasn't well articulated, but it was obvious when we hit it. This rule was often self-enforced by the kids, because we thought complaining might add to Mom's burdens, that complaints might make her sad. This was one of our biggest fears and motivators, then and throughout childhood—

not making Mom sad. We thought of it precisely that way, that it was us who could make her sad. We rarely considered that there was a greater sadness, one that was not our doing, and that the small frustrations we caused only seemed massive because they led our mom to a cul-de-sac filled with more complex emotions. This sadness wasn't obvious back then, because we never talked about it. Ever.

The only homework rule I recall was that we had to do it. Academic achievement was not stressed, partly out of fear of committing the sin of pride and partly as a way to even out any differences in children. We hadn't grasped the notion that each child might be brilliant in his or her own way, so we tended to ignore brilliance, if and when it arose. When report cards were sent home, the A's and B's were nice, but the only grades Mom really commented on were the ones given for conduct and effort. Success just wasn't valued in our house; who you were and who you were becoming mattered more than what you accomplished. The work itself, and the fact that you did it, that you tried, was what mattered.

We had chores, but they never seemed a burden. It may be that we had never known otherwise, but it more likely was a benefit of being in a large family, with many hands available. I tended the lawns, mowing and raking as needed, and took out the garbage. I emptied the dishwasher, which we purchased when adding on to the house. The chores rarely got in the way of fun. Grass fights and leaf fights were regular occurrences. Raked into piles, the detritus would be ammunition, the California equivalent of a stack of snowballs. After a spring battle, we could have blades of grass in the folds of our clothes and stuck to our shoes for days; we simply moved an outside mess indoors. If it was a night heavy with homework—rare for me, but less so for the more conscientious sisters—it was easy to find someone to do the chores; we covered for each other and traded chores often.

We were not to seek sympathy from people outside the family. More expressly, we were not to exploit any sympathy people might feel for us. With Terry now in the eighth grade, parties might include both boys and girls. She was about to be excluded from one, hosted by the Lovisco twins, Patty and Ellen. With a strategy not well designed, she told Mom she had been excluded because the party somehow involved fathers and daughters. She wondered if Mom might call Mrs. Lovisco to see if Terry could perhaps be invited. Mom called, found that her daughter had simply been stiffed as any kid might be, and made it clear to Terry that she would not be going to this party or the next.

The only rule regarding television was that it had to be off during dinner. That was it. *Rowan & Martin's Laugh-In* was the most popular show in America when I was a fourth grader, and we never missed an episode. *Bonanza* was still a Sunday evening staple. Each weeknight, at least one child had a favorite show or two, so the television was always on. Two or three of us would sit, with books and notepads on our laps, watching television and doing our homework.

Mom had her own chair, a recliner, and none of us were to

sit in it. It was relatively expensive and needed to last twenty years, which it did. We sat in it often, of course, usually when Mom was out, but Pat would occasionally sit in it when she was home. He happily took a quarter from his pocket and handed it to Mom as he pushed back to recline. It seemed to be his version of a T-bone steak, something I think our mother grasped. We were to kiss our mother every time we left the house for an extended period. It was demanded as a sign of respect, I suppose, but it never felt affectionate. The quick buss on the cheek had little impact, except maybe to slowly diminish the prospect that we might be a family of real hugs. We were close as a family but didn't hold each other. We just didn't touch. There was no married couple to lead the way now—ours was a house void of sex and passion—and whatever sensual connections might have been bottled up six years earlier when Daddy died had stayed put.

Our mom was now working, as the attendance clerk at Peninsula High School, an alternative school that had been built on the old navy base. The pay was meager, but the job fit Mom's two most important criteria. Because it went from eight o'clock until two, she was home to send us off to school in the morning, would be home by the time any of us returned, and had summers off. Just as important, her new job provided family health insurance. We had gone months without it and were put on the rolls just in the nick of time. Only days after Mom took her new job, Kathy fell off the back of a bicycle. She had been riding double by standing on the wheel axles, and slipped, scraping her face horribly, and leaving half a front tooth somewhere on Sycamore Avenue. The insurance covered emergency room costs, but it was years before we could afford a cap for her chipped tooth. Kathy spent half of her childhood looking like the world's cutest hockey player: a skinny little girl with red pigtails, a few freckles, and half a front tooth.

The days when I was home sick from school are when I most noticed that Mom held a job. Even if I really was sick, these days tended to be good ones. If one of us was ill, odds were good that another was ill as well. There was half a week when three of us were home at once. Terry had the German measles, I had the mumps, and Aileen was laid up with two broken arms—on the previous Saturday, she had fallen in a Cypress Avenue skateboard race. The television was on all day, and we played games endlessly. Too sick and sore to make it to school, we were in good health while Mom was out. By the time she got home, of course, we were exhausted and our illnesses had caught up with us. We needed Mom's care, each of us, right then.

The summer after I finished fourth grade was the last year our whole family, all seven of us, vacationed together. Pat was already saving for college. (If any of us were to attend—not a foregone conclusion—we had to pay for it entirely on our own.) We knew by this point that a week away from work was not a luxury Pat could again afford.

We packed all we could fit into our family's pink Chevy

station wagon. (Mom chose a pink car from the used car lot because she knew it would be easy to find it in a crowded parking lot. Unknowingly, she taught us that choices based strictly on practicality could misfire.) Each of us jammed a week's worth of clothing, a towel, and a few other items into our own cardboard box, scavenged from behind Zanetti's Liquors; we tied several of these to the top of the car. It was a familiar routine, because we went to the same place every year. I never yearned to go elsewhere. Ben Lomond was as much a home to us as Cypress Avenue.

The drive was harrowing. Our car would not make it up and over the hill that was the most direct path, so we took a circuitous route, hugging the cliffs along the Pacific Ocean. Heavy winds buffeted the boxes on top, and we stopped several times to make sure things were secure. Pat was our driver, though he was still new at the task; it was better him than Mom, though I didn't quite know why. Our arrival was never certain because of our car's unreliability, but when we made it to the town of Santa Cruz, all was well. The rest of the drive was flat, and if the car didn't make it, we were close enough that we might still get there on our own. We backtracked north, following the canyon of the San Lorenzo River. At the time, I could identify only two native trees with confidence—coastal live oaks and redwoods—and the drive was filled with both. The canyon grew dark as the redwoods shot up, and I leaned my head out the window to take in the smell of the moist red bark. It was a primal feel; I was a Californian and these were my trees. Back then, I knew only the general categories of the birds I saw—ducks and hawks and songbirds—but I gasped to myself when I saw the varieties and all their colors.

We passed the covered bridge at Felton, and turned onto Old County Road, in the tiny hamlet of Ben Lomond. We stretched ourselves and adjusted to the light as we unloaded from the car. A woodpecker sounded somewhere in the mass of trees.

The Ahdina Cabins were set in a cluster of buildings: four rental cabins, the Beach family's home (Joe and Muriel Beach owned the place), and two cottages—one for Grandma Beach and one for Grandma Monaghan, the Beach family matriarchs. They were arranged in a circle around shuffleboard courts, a Ping-Pong table, and lawn chairs. For one week, we rented cabin number one, with its two rooms plus bath. All six kids crowded into one room, with two bunks, a twin bed, and a crib; Kathy, though nearly seven, was still consigned to the crib. Our mother slept on a cot in the other room, which also happened to be the kitchen.

The river was dammed in the summer, creating a huge swimming hole near the town center. We swam much of the day, scaling the steep hillside that formed one bank to use the rope swing that hung from an oak branch leaning over the water. We had soft ice creams in the middle of the afternoon, and if Mom wasn't there to buy the round, Pat was. Every weekday at four, a bagpiper started on his rounds, playing the pipes and walking the gravel roads that wound through the forest. Sounds from the pipes echoed off the canyon walls or bounced off redwoods, so it was hard to find him, but we always did, instantly falling in line to march behind him. This was a tradition in the town, and some years we got to know the player. That year, the summer of 1968, his name was Sandy, and he was a student at San Diego State; like every other player before him, he was the best. We may have been children of Irish descent, but we loved the Scottish enclave of Ben Lomond, and we were grateful to whichever Scot had paid the piper. In the evenings, we played basketball, shuffleboard or Ping-Pong, and sat around an outdoor fire in an open pit. We walked down to the river and breathed in redwoods in the darkness. An auntie or uncle usually came down for a day, to ferry us into Santa Cruz and spring for rides on the boardwalk—roller coaster and bumper cars for the lot of us.

It was familiar and safe. We knew people in town and they knew us, and it seemed we'd run into a Beach kid or one of their grandmas any time we strolled about. It was yet another place where we felt protected, special even. We were treated like family, and the Beach parents sat with our mom for hours, having cocktails and talking about the year gone by. It was clear that they loved her and enjoyed her company. But they had known our father, too—we had been visiting for years even before he died—and it felt like they were looking out for us. The price of the cabin never increased for our family; it was ours, for a week, for seventy dollars.

My childhood would have been utterly different without those vacations. They offered a stability and calmness I didn't know I needed. I didn't know then that there were traps—land mines really—that were bound to go off if they weren't defused.

8

The Prospect of Snow

While ten years old and in the fifth grade, I took on a paper route with the *San Mateo Times.* The route my brother delivered years earlier had been divided in two after he left it for his job at Zanetti's, and I now had what amounted to roughly half of his load. This gave Pat cause to tease, an opportunity he embraced often. As we grew older, our words took on a more sarcastic tone, with teasing now the main form of affection we showed each other. The willingness to help out, to do things for each other, to be there physically and to work alongside each other never lapsed, but any chance we had to speak tenderly about hardships or worries or loves had, it seemed, already passed us by. In this case, Pat had earned the right to say what he wanted; the route never would have been mine had he not preceded me.

Acquiring a paper route was no lark. These were treasured possessions, like New York City taxi medallions, and could be passed down within the same family for years, from brother to brother to cousin to a neighbor who understood that it would go back to the original family. The passing down was tolerated, even encouraged, by the *Times,* so long as the job continued to be done well. If a family tended toward irresponsibility, the district manager would snatch the route and give it to someone else on the long list of boys awaiting prosperity. But if a good delivery boy wished to hand it over to a relative, old Mr. Speaker— the *Times*'s district manager for San Bruno—would let him do it, trusting in genetic predictability. When Lennie Bettencourt had grown tired of the route that had once been delivered faithfully by a Sweeney, it was all right with Mr. Speaker and all right with the *Times* if Lennie wanted to give it over to Pat's little brother.

I was now employed. It wasn't just that I had a paper route; this was my first job. I knew when I took it that it was not just the beginning of work; I knew then that there would never be another period in my life when I didn't work. In the fifth grade, I could see, as clear as daylight, that this was my destiny. I would be saving money right away to attend Serra High School, the all-male Catholic school that my mother and I both wanted me to attend, but which she could not afford on her own; if I was to attend Serra, I would pay for at least half. After helping to pay for high school, I would need to save for college, and once in college, I would need to continue working. And then there would be the rest of life—and men worked. So this was it, and I knew it. Whether I was ready or not wasn't really the issue, though. The route was available right then; the only relevant question was whether I would take it or let it slip forever into another family, into an unfriendly line of brothers, cousins, and friends. I couldn't complain about this, of course; I couldn't express frustration about my lot. That would come too close to sadness, too close to that room we could not enter. When work became a burden, then, I was more comfortable with anger and righteousness. I was better than the boys who didn't work. I knew then that the phrase *I've been working since I was ten* would be a source of pride for me, a weapon, even. And, really, I had that job, the miniroute, when I was six, I would tell myself.

The work did have its immediate rewards. I was now independent, able to afford things I wanted or needed, and I liked that.

I delivered to forty-two homes, a number that increased slightly over the next four years. Most days I folded papers while sitting on the living room floor, listening to the older kids' albums—Simon & Garfunkel, The Mommas & The Poppas, The Beatles, and The Association. With stacks of papers arranged in a crescent around me, I looped dozens of rubber bands over my left index finger, made one-third folds in the paper with each hand, and stretched a band over the folded newspaper, all in one motion. Even with advertising inserts to stash inside, I could fold and fasten six to ten papers a minute. I stuffed all of the papers into a canvas delivery bag that I usually strapped to my bike's handlebars.

Papers needed to be placed on the porch. Not the walkway, lawn, or one of the steps—that was not how it was done. I was to make it possible for a customer to open the front door and simply reach down to grab the day's news. This was so much a part of my job then—quality work. The goal was clearly defined as the porch, right in front of the door. If I didn't hit the mark, I stopped, got off my bike, and made it right. And if I didn't do so, odds were good that the customer would point it out later in the week. "Hey Red! How 'bout getting it on the porch, all right?" How it reached the porch was also an issue. Screen doors were easily dented—and made a huge noise—when hit with a newspaper. The stucco on the neighborhood homes could be scuffed and marked with newsprint if the paper was flung too hard. It was a delicate and graceful art form, this practice of riding my bike at a fast clip and gently tossing a paper on a much slower trajectory. A high arc and backspin were key in transferring momentum away from the door and wall, down into the porch. A good toss could be known by its sound. A simple "plop!" meant it had fallen gently and with a steep angle, with the paper barely moving from its original placement. "Ka-plop!" could also signal a good toss; again, it meant the throw's energy had been borne into the porch. Anything more, though, and I would know to either stop and take a look—or to ride on quickly, avoiding the prospect of eye contact with a customer whose wall had been scarred temporarily by newsprint.

The drop-dead delivery time was five o'clock, when, in Mom's words, "all the men are home from work and want their papers now." If a customer called the *Times* to complain about a late paper, it cost me money, because the *Times* added one dollar to my "Junior Merchant Bank Account" for each month without a complaint. (If I found new customers for the route, which I rarely did, the *Times* would also kick in an additional dollar.)

That money mattered greatly, because for twenty-nine Junior Merchant dollars, I could buy a spot on the *Times* annual trip to Disneyland. An airplane ride to and from Los Angeles, a bus ride to Disneyland, and a book full of tickets, leaving home at seven in the morning and not getting home until nine at night. No mom, no sisters—just me and fifty other paperboys, all of whom purchased rubber bands in bags of a thousand or more. I could not afford to miss out, so I stopped customers from calling the *Times* by giving them my home phone number. "Call me if there's ever a problem," I said. Because there were problems, they called me. If Mom answered the phone, or if she found out that a customer had complained, the reproach, though never shouted or prolonged, was harsh. Dependability was important to her. Not letting people down was important. At times, I felt awful, believing I had let my mom down. But by this age, I also felt anger. It was all too much. It was my job, they were my customers, and any consequences were mine. I could learn whatever lessons I needed to learn on my own. It was none of her business, I could tell myself. I couldn't know then that she was not really talking to me in those moments when she expressed anger or disappointment. I couldn't know because we never talked about the man she was addressing.

Although there was pressure to deliver on time six days a week, there was also the cash. At month's end, I knocked on forty-two doors, with a refrain of "Collecting for the *Times*." With ten dollars in tips, I earned forty-five dollars a month. The process of coaxing a tip was an important skill. "Let me get you some change," I said, taking ten seconds or so to fumble around in my right pocket. With quarters always in the left pocket and smaller coins always in the right, I reliably pulled out only pennies, nickels, and dimes, then sorted for the right change. It was enough time for a decent wage earner to say, "Keep the change," or to at least contemplate whether or not they should kick in an extra quarter for the redhead who usually did an okay job. If I knew a tip was coming anyway, I would have the exact change in hand, visibly poised to turn it over immediately. This ritual allowed me to be surprised, every month, by a customer's generosity. To act as if I expected such treatment, as if I took it all for granted, would have felt sinful. And simply saying "thank you" for a tip didn't seem like enough.

After that first month, I had a bank account and made regular deposits. After a few more months, I had a new baseball mitt and spikes. Later in the year, I owned baseball bats of my own. There was no longer a visible difference between me and the other kids at St. Robert's or in San Bruno. I had what most kids my age had. The only difference—and I was aware of the difference—was that I had paid for much of it myself.

Year-round, we played football and baseball games right there on the street. In touch football, the lamppost was one goal line, the Fanucchis' tree the other. These games rarely involved more than three on a side, but one could find additional teammates by deftly using a parked car as a screen. We occasionally played knee football, using a strip of lawn no more than fifteen feet long. Players could not leave their knees, making it a harmless exercise where neither skill nor speed had any bearing. After half an hour of knee football, there would be no difference between the street's good athletes and its poor ones. It was a particularly good game for me. I was a competent athlete and made smart plays, but I simply wasn't fast enough to keep up with Ricky Garban or the older boys.

Team baseball games were played on the dead end of Magnolia Avenue; any baseball games on Cypress were played one-on-one. The field of play flowed across the street, from one side to the other—usually from our house to the Flicks. One player pitched a tennis ball against the garage door, and if the batter missed or if the ball hit the square taped to the door, it was a strike. A hit ball fielded cleanly by the pitcher was called an out.

The goal was to hit the ball sharply on the ground, shooting it past the pitcher before he could react. There were significant risks to hitting the ball in the air. If a hit ball sailed over a roof across the street, it was a home run—the batter had taken a risk, hit it cleanly, and should be rewarded. But if it touched any part of the roof or if it hit any of the house's painted trim, the batter was out. If a ball hit a window, the whole inning was over. And if the window was broken, the game was over.

One of the times I broke a window on our house's front bedroom, I knew the key was to move quickly.

Ricky Garban and I used flat-edged screwdrivers to scrape out the dried glazing and remove any shards still stuck in the frame. We measured the size of the window from the outside.

There weren't parents around to drive to the lumber company, so it was a long walk to pick up the glass that the men there had cut to order. By the time we got home, the panic had subsided and the fun work began. Now into the finesse part of the job, we had been through this before, helping out as older boys had mended other broken windows. We had used glazing compound many times and were confident replacing windows of almost any size. By our age—I was ten and Ricky was eleven—if you couldn't glaze a window, you weren't much of a hitter or you weren't taking risks. We focused on moving at a steady pace, trying to finish the job before any dads got home. If we pulled that off, the conversation would gravitate to the quality of the work, not to the fact that we had broken a window in the first place. When Mr. Fanucchi showed up first, we were home free: He never cared a whit about which kid broke the glass, but he was a fanatic for a good window job.

Mr. Fanucchi was the best fix-it-quickly dad on our street. He usually did repairs—on broken windows, doors, drawers, or cabinets—on his own while the kids watched, but if one of us boys had taken care of it, he derived immense pleasure. As he took in the repair job Ricky and I had done, he was all smiles, all compliments. A few of the other dads showed up to look at the work. An incident that had started with my heart in my throat, with the shattering of my sister's bedroom window, had ended with me and a few other guys—most of them men in their forties—talking about the various ways we fixed things.

Ricky and I had done much of the work together, but because it was my house, I was in charge. My first real window job, and it was said to be a fine one. I wasn't yet eleven, but it wouldn't have surprised me if Mr. Fanucchi offered me a beer. That's how big I felt. One of the men.

I was aware that I did not remember my father. I was aware, or so I thought, that I could not miss him if I didn't remember him. I was aware that my mom had said—many times to people outside of our family who had suffered the loss of a loved one— that it takes a good three years to really move on. When eight years had passed since my father's death, there was nothing to feel anymore, at least not in my case.

But there was.

There was an annual buildup in our house prior to February first, the anniversary of our father's death. It started in mid-January, after the holidays were done and we were back to our daily routines. Every year, we expected sadness, or at least solemnity. It was our mother's sadness, not ours, not the children's, that we anticipated. We kept the house clean and noise to a minimum. We said dinnertime grace deliberately, as if it was Daddy's bounty, not Christ's, which we were about to receive. We helped one another with chores, making sure to offer our help aloud, so Mom might know of our kindness. We would do nothing to cause our mother to be sad, and if we weren't quite the cause, we would do nothing to increase her burden. In the days before and after the anniversary, starting a fight or argument would have been unconscionable, worthy of banishment by my sisters.

"Mom does not need this right now," one of them would say to me in reproach. This was not something our mother asked for; it was something we did, feeling our way along an unknown path.

We didn't talk about how horrible that day had once been. We didn't talk about Grandma's dress and how it changed colors. We didn't talk about the doctors who failed then but who could have saved him if he had held out another few years, partly from what they learned opening up our daddy instead of someone else's. We didn't talk about how penicillin could have prevented the rheumatic fever, if only his strep throat had come six years later, when the antibiotic came into use, saving the lives of thousands of fathers—maybe millions of fathers. We never talked about it. We never talked about him. On this day in particular, we consciously avoided any of the words that might trigger grief or sadness. Six young children, like nuns gliding silently in the vestry.

On the day itself, we attended mass together at St. Robert's. A seven o'clock weekday Mass, and we joined the elderly women who were daily communicants. During the canon, just after the consecration of the body and blood, the priest made eye contact with us as he said the prayer for the dead. Why else would a whole family but one be there on a Tuesday morning? "Remember, Lord, all the angels and saints and all the dearly departed who have gone before us in your mercy." One year—I don't recall which year—Father Flynn actually said aloud, "including our departed brother Jim Sweeney." It was at this moment, when words were uttered about my father, that I felt an overwhelming sadness and began to cry in public. Only for a moment and only once, but I cried in church over my father's death. The generic phrase struck me each year on this day, whether Daddy was mentioned aloud or not. *All the angels and saints and all the dearly departed who have gone before us in your mercy.* I heard the phrase on thousands of Sundays, but when I heard it on February first, I would know deep inside that Jim Sweeney had walked the earth and was with us no more. Like Jesus, like the saints, my daddy was born, suffered, and died. The saints had become human, my daddy a saint.

That would be it, though, that one moment in church. Aside from that, February first was like most days. It was hard to isolate my sadness, to know it, confront it, or even realize it existed. It was the dead of winter, the rains would keep falling for another month or more, our house was cold and our father was dead. I couldn't wallow in his death without attaching it to something else. It had become part of the general sadness, the world's sadness.

I could not feel sad over my father's death when I was supposed to. But the sadness did come, on its own.

For my sisters, it showed up in the weeks before father-daughter dances. Those were the school gatherings at which girls who had not yet fallen into the spell of adolescent rebellion stared into their fathers' eyes while dancing to recorded music. At least that's how I imagined they were. What I knew for a fact was that they brought on bouts of immense frustration for my sisters. These were supposed to be the easy dates, the dates at which girls got used to waiting for a door to be opened, to walking into a party holding a man's hand, to being asked to dance over and over, to being taken to Farrell's for ice cream on the way home. For the Sweeney girls, these dances instead started with the excruciating task of figuring out which dad—which other person's dad—they would ask as their date. These were the dances where they learned, long before their classmates and long before they should have, that dating was not always easy. There were gracious men in our community who squired Jim Sweeney's daughters, and in some cases they stepped forward to ask on their own—not waiting to make a teenage girl say the words aloud. It was a horrible thing to watch, and each of my sisters went through it. Anne would not show sadness in these cases, but was angry, and it was one of the few times when I could see—in someone else, of course—that the anger had its roots in sadness. I was saddened deeply as I watched my sisters go through these rituals.

It showed up in my sister Aileen's dreams. Hers were the wildest dreams I had ever heard described. Women floating outside the window, their gowns billowing in wind currents all lit up in brilliant colors. And death, lots and lots of death. This wasn't a young girl telling stories to get attention; she would awaken all of us in the middle of the night with her screams, remaining visibly shaken for half an hour or more. There was the knife-is-breaking-skin scream, the car-is-about-to-hit-the-child scream, the man-is-really-in-the-closet-he-really-is-there scream. There were times when it was funny. We awoke one morning to find a bedroom window wide open—even though it had been painted shut years earlier. But there it was, the open window, with the curtains billowing in the breeze and the muddy footprints of a fifteen-year-old girl up the wall; she opened it to save her little sister in the yard. There was nothing in the yard that night, of course, so Aileen walked the muddy grass in darkness before climbing back into her room and bed. There was the time she moved our piano across the living room carpet, believing her godson had fallen behind it. It took several of us working together to push the piano back in place. We marveled at her strength and we joked about it often, but on the nights of her screams, we all returned to bed troubled. She was walking the nineteen steps in her sleep, but didn't know it. We never put it all together back then, or those who did couldn't explain it to us. I never heard anyone suggest that the dreams might be connected to the sudden loss of a loved one, that they might betray a deep-seated fear or sadness. The only thing I knew then was that my sister was braver, by far, than any of us, with the possible exception of our mother. Not in a million years would I have opened all the closet doors she opened, even after hearing my dear sister's screams.

For me, the sadness came when a massive cold front sliding down from the Gulf of Alaska collided with a warmer, moister storm racing up from the South Pacific.

When I was eleven, weather forecasters announced the possibility of snow in San Bruno. The overnight lows would be in the twenties, and there was a 30 percent chance of snow. The mere chance of snow made our friends delirious. The talk everywhere was of what kids would do if and when it snowed. Everywhere it seemed, except for our house. It never did snow again, at least not outside. But the prospect came every few years.

More than anything else in my life, it was the prospect of snow on Cypress Avenue that would send me, barefoot and unknowing, into the cold, dark canyons of my own sadness. It had snowed on Daddy's last day home. Snow was the last good thing that would happen in our life with him. By this point, I may have thought it was the only good thing. And he died eight days later. The thought of snow was unbearable, causing a blizzard of white noise and confusion for me. I couldn't focus on objects or words or ideas that lay there in front of me. I couldn't talk of this with anyone—my friends were too happy with the prospect, and I didn't dare break the family's silent code of avoiding words that could bring forth sadness or pain. I couldn't do that to the others. I couldn't do it to myself—I had no idea what would happen if I opened up and talked about how I felt. I wanted to ask about the day he died, how he died, why he died. I just wanted to say something, to hear something, to do something to expose whatever it was that was in me right then. I needed to speak and was too afraid to do so. It was stifling, and confusing.

It was not the cemetery, or February first, or his birthday, or any of the predictable days or places that would cause me to break down. It was the prospect of snow that marked the passing of time without my daddy. I stayed in my room, or whatever room in the house was empty, until the storm had passed.

9
Fundamentally Sound

My search for a third dad, for a third man to show me the way, did not consume me. A back-burner process, I tended to it only occasionally. Had I worked harder at the search, though, the time would likely have been wasted. The third dad was sitting behind us in church, usually two or three rows back, and had been there every Sunday for several years.

Sherm Heaney worked with my uncle Bill, Mom's younger brother, at the Crown Zellerbach Paper Company. Both men were Catholic boys from San Francisco, USF graduates, and company men, staying with Zellerbach and its later incarnations for their entire professional lives. Both started in sales, moving later into jobs that blended sales and marketing. Uncle Bill moved his family to southern California when I was ten; a better Zellerbach job awaited, and he could leave the San Francisco fog behind. After their move, when the Fallons visited our house, other families occasionally dropped by, and on one of those trips, when I was twelve, the Heaneys came by: Sherm, Dee, and their four kids. Their son Dennis was a year younger than me, and after a few visits in the context of Fallon gatherings, he and I became good friends, hanging out often on our own. Dennis would be one of my best friends from that point through high school.

Sherm was physically graceful. A three-sport star in high school, he played basketball at USF. Bill Russell and K.C. Jones trailed him by three years at the school and would go on to the Boston Celtics and the NBA Hall of Fame. Sherm was not on USF's national championship team with them, but he played the same game on the same court with many of the same players, and I imagined then that he taught the younger stars a thing or two about defense. We heard none of this from Sherm—he was too understated for that—but my mom and uncle told me the stories.

Sherm was noticeable then for his friendliness. While the other dads followed the axiom that started with "If you can't say anything nice," Sherm was someone who actually *could* say something nice. It seemed he always had something nice to say—or at least something respectful. Though I came to expect it, I never grew tired of it. He was a genuinely nice man, with a real interest in others. He was conscious of his approach, once telling me, "It's easy to find the negative. I just don't feel like looking for it."

On occasional Sundays, Sherm was the lector at the 9:00 mass, reading the Epistle, Responsorial Psalm, and Prayer of the Faithful. I loved when he read at mass. Some in our parish read in studied fashion, bringing drama to the Bible and filling the text with long pauses. A few read the words of the prophets the way they thought a prophet might actually speak. Sherm just read. He stood before the crowd and softly read the story, as if he had just picked up the Book and found a passage he wanted to share with us. It felt as if he had just said, "Say, here's a neat story, listen to this one." The drama was already there, and Sherm knew enough to know that he was simply a conveyance. I don't recall exactly, but I suspect it was on a Sunday that I adopted him.

Theirs was an easy house to visit. The kitchen opened up to a family room, the room of choice for playing at the Heaneys. Dee was in the kitchen and would waltz in and out of our conversations—when visiting the Heaneys, you were part of the family, and most boundaries were tossed aside. The family room was also where the television was, and after he golfed on Saturday mornings, we might watch a game with Sherm. He noticed things the announcer didn't pick up—a block, a pick, or someone dropping back to help defend the weak side. He wasn't loud or overbearing in doing this, but the banter had its impact: His son Dennis was the most fundamentally sound athlete I would ever play with on a court or field. It was more than just sports, of course. In anything they did, the Heaneys seemed like a family that found the open man, that followed their shots, that hit behind the runner. They did the little things. They did things right. At the time, I tried to follow Sherm's advice on the court. I was not a gifted athlete, but it was Sherm who pointed out that if you could play good defense, well, there would always be a spot for you. The greater lesson, though, was in knowing how a game was played, in how something was done well.

He was a dad we could tease. Sherm had served in U.S. Army Intelligence after the war, during the American occupation of Japan, and the Heaney kids dragged out his army pictures. Here's a photo of Sherm playing basketball in Japan. There's another of him playing softball. "It was hard work," he said. "Rough stuff. But we had to find creative ways to preserve the peace." He smiled and went back to reading the newspaper.

Just after I turned twelve, I stayed with Grandma and Grandpa Sweeney for a few days, right before seventh grade was to start. I still held Grandpa's hand as we went for our walks. I would have been embarrassed to do so in San Bruno—boys my age weren't supposed to hold hands with men—but we were in the city, far away from people who might recognize me. He was eighty-two, his step continued to slow, and I held his hand to steady him. It also felt good, it felt close, to be touching him.

On the Sunday morning when I was to go home, he walked around the downstairs part of his house, taking things out of cabinets or off shelves, examining them and handing them to me. The sweet smell of his pipe filled the downstairs as we moved slowly through the basement. There was a sword, with Japanese writing on it, that my father must have brought home from the South Pacific. There was an ornate wooden club, probably from a Pacific Island; it, too, had been my father's. Then he held the carved, wooden ship I had spent hours examining as a child, a model of an ocean liner, perhaps the one on which Grandpa had sailed to America. It was kept in a large glass case, and we occasionally plugged in the cord to see electric lights shining through tiny portholes. It was made by his old, dead friend, Axel, a Swedish sailor who lived in Grandpa's rooming house. The ship was given when Axel was unable to pay his rent. We placed the pile of treasures on the downstairs dresser, and Grandpa, who did little more than mumble when smoking his pipe, said his good-bye. "I want you to have these, boy. I want you to have them."

Grandpa had a stroke a few weeks later and was incapacitated until his death that November. It was hard not to imagine that he knew what would happen, that he knew he was about to die.

His funeral was like so many others we had attended through the years. With such a large extended family, and having roots so deep in Bay Area soils, we knew a great many old people. And those old people were dying all the time. We had been through the rosaries, the wakes, the funeral masses. We had been to the homes afterward and could muster up the courage to say a kind word to the elderly widow or widower. It was just something we did growing up.

Grandpa's funeral was different, but not in the way I expected. We had a blast. We played touch football in the park across from the funeral home after saying a rosary by his coffin. At his house after the funeral, kids filled the downstairs and backyard—siblings, cousins, family friends. We ran and laughed and even stole sips of beer. At some point, my feelings began to shift. I felt guilty—Grandpa was freshly buried at Holy Cross Cemetery and I had sipped beer. I felt sad—I could still smell his tobacco throughout the basement and wondered how long it would linger. So I began to act as one is supposed to act at a funeral. That's when Uncle Roger stepped in, pulling my cousin, Kevin Desler, and me aside, sitting us down in one of the bedrooms.

"There'll be no sad faces here, you hear me?" Roger said. "This is a celebration. It's fun. It's okay to have fun. Your grandfather lived to be eighty-two, and that's a good thing. God knows, in this family, it's a very good thing. So we can tell stories about him. We can remember the good times and the bad. But for God's sake, don't go moping around."

Roger was right, in that we had cause to be grateful—our Grandpa had lived a long life. But I missed him already, and I was aware of it. I still miss Grandpa Sweeney.

———————————

On a Saturday night that year, Mom's St. Cecilia's girlfriends were over for their annual winter gathering; they would stay late into the evening. When Alice joined the crowd, Jim Gaffney and their son Greg, who was my age, also stepped in. After exchanging greetings with the women and before asking my mom, Jim leaned over and whispered to me.

"There's a lot of women in here," he said. "Do you want to come with us?"

We left without saying where we were headed, only that we'd be back later.

The three of us went to see a movie, and it wasn't a matinee—it was a first run movie on a Saturday night. With sodas, candy, and popcorn spilling over our laps, we bore witness as the Japanese bombed Pearl Harbor in *Tora! Tora! Tora!* It was all boys, all strategy and bombs and shouting, and I loved every minute of it. Picking out an ice cream flavor at Shaw's afterward was barely a distraction. "Why didn't Stanton listen to the warnings? Why? I'll have thin mint, dipped, please. It was all so obvious, and they missed it."

I still craved time with the three fathers, still watched how they carried themselves, still listened to the words they chose and thought about why they might have chosen them. I saw two of my dads at basketball games during the year. When St. Robert's played St. Tim's, where the Kelly kids went to school, Chick arrived early for Neil's game, perhaps intending to catch the tail end of mine. He stood at the end of the court in his peacoat, not moving to the tiny row of seats, looking as if he wanted no distractions, as if he couldn't miss a thing. At St. Pius, Greg Gaffney and I played against each other on the same court, an almost indescribable pleasure, nearly as much fun and as loaded as playing against a cousin. The Gaffneys sat with Mom then, and as the two women talked nonstop, Jim stared intently at the game, smiling at the plays his boys were making.

That summer, the Gaffneys invited us to vacation with

them at Lake Tahoe. The three younger children—Anne, Kathy, and I—joined the Gaffneys, while the older kids—Pat, Aileen, and Terry—stayed home to work at summer jobs. I found a temporary replacement for my paper route.

I was twelve now and had not yet been out of California, and the condo the Gaffneys used was on the lake's north side, a few miles into Nevada. On its own, for the sheer joy of crossing the state line, that would have been worth the long drive.

We rode on a glass-bottomed boat, pee-wee golfed, and drank sodas whenever we cared to. We toured the Ponderosa Ranch, where *Bonanza* was filmed, and Jim let us pick out anything we wanted from the ranch's general store. When I selected a tin cup with a picture of the three Cartwright boys on it, Jim shrugged, as if to suggest that, really, I could have picked out something a little more expensive. Still, he put it on the pile of booty at the register. The wealth and whatever luxuries it afforded were not what I sought on the trip, though. I played with Greg, Jeff, and the other Gaffney kids. I swam in the icy cold lake. And I watched the cool and elegant Jim Gaffney.

I saw him discipline his children. He didn't quite raise his voice—or when he did, it seemed more that he was acting the part, that he was showing them he might really get angry. There was enough behind it that we took notice and found ways to calm ourselves. He insisted that his children be polite. When a visitor stopped by and one of the kids didn't get up to greet her, he raised an eyebrow and stared. I remember a moment when Jeff got the picture. He stood up, said hello to the visitor, and looked directly into her eyes as he asked how she was doing, staying with the conversation long enough to make her feel welcomed. Not a quick handshake or buss on the cheek, it was a genuine welcome. Jeff felt good, Jim thanked him, and, though Marian Sweeney's children were all polite, I had learned even more about the art of being a gracious and polite young man. Later in the week, when we were asking for directions at a casino, Greg addressed a young woman as "Miss." I had never before heard the term used in real conversation.

Jim and Alice touched each other often, hugging, kissing, and flirting with each other. They were grown-ups, but he made her giggle with jokes no one else heard.

He spent time on the beach with Alice and my mom. I suppose if my dad had been around, or if other men were present, the genders might have separated, but what I noticed then was Jim sitting with the two women on the beach. If drinks needed filling or the chip bowl was empty, it was always Jim who went inside for refills. He delivered with a flourish—drinks in fresh glasses and garnished, and a napkin resting on his arm as he served. He cooked breakfast every day on vacation, and when he sat down at last to eat, he ate his bacon with a fork. My sisters and I tried not to stare; we just assumed everyone ate bacon with their fingers.

He required his own time and insisted on lengthy stretches where he could sit quietly by the lake, reading or watching the kids swim and play. The beach was not crowded—it was a private beach, after all—but had it been so, it looked as if he could have found his own peace and quiet with a thousand people around him. The lake, the pines, and the mountains were all big enough to calm him. Or perhaps it was just him, calming all that surrounded him.

By this time, I was tired of living with women. My brother had been off at college for three years, and our home was now filled with Mom, four girls, and me. Their voices, needs, and wants grated on me, and there were days—weeks, even—when I wanted out. I was feeling this again, though we were in Tahoe with the Gaffneys, as we waited to drive around the lake. The girls had gotten ready, then got ready again, then needed something else. While I felt myself getting angry, Jim looked patient. Immensely patient. He didn't seem to mind what I saw as the roller coaster of female emotions. A commotion didn't have to affect him.

"Let's play catch," he said, leaning over the porch rail to grab a football. We tossed the ball around, and as the delay grew longer and longer, we started running plays. Greg was guarding me closely on a hook-and-go, and when I sprinted long with everything I had, a neat spiral fell from the sky onto my fingertips. I cradled the ball in my arms as I ran on the narrow, asphalt drive lined with towering Jeffery pines. The pines smelled great, the wind brushed my face, and the anger had passed.

We vacationed with the Gaffneys the following year, again sharing their condo at Lake Tahoe. Nearly two full weeks, all told, under the same roof with one of my chosen fathers—I was learning how.

At twelve and thirteen, few things in my life approached the importance of baseball. I may have had a typical relationship with the national pastime, no different than many American boys at the time, but proximity to San Francisco meant I was raised in the dominion of Willie Mays, the greatest ballplayer ever. It affected me.

Youth baseball teams would go as one to a Giants game or two each year, with the coach telling kids to pick out one player to watch closely for the entire game. "Don't just watch the hitter," he would say. "Watch how the outfielders position themselves. Watch the shortstop's footwork." We all watched Willie Mays.

My generation of San Franciscans is uniquely optimistic because of Willie Mays. The Giants finished second five years in a row, right about the time when my arc of love for baseball was cresting. We were heartbroken in September, but the standings, really, didn't matter. Every time we went to Candlestick Park, something magical happened. His hat flew off as he raced for a fly ball. He might not get a hit, but he drew a walk, rattled the pitcher, and caused the mistake that led to a McCovey home run. He guessed where a hitter would send the ball based on the pitch the catcher called and was leaning there before the swing was complete. We knew that winning was nice and something to strive for, but we also saw that playing well, perhaps even with flourish, made for a good life. The outcome, which we could not control, was never the sole source of our joy.

I had played for years already and was competent defensively. A fundamentally sound first baseman on most teams, I knew how to shift my feet into position to make a relay throw, let nothing get past me, and took great pleasure in calling "time" to chat with the pitcher when it appeared he needed a distraction. But I couldn't hit. Not at all. I struck out more often than not, and when I managed to hit the ball, it rarely went far or fast.

Many men tried to teach me hitting, and each failed, just as I failed nearly every time I stepped to the plate. In the sixth grade, Mr. Mitchell went to great lengths to stop me from stepping away from a pitch. After I took my position in the batter's box, he placed himself prone on the ground behind me, his legs and feet stretching away, his arms reaching out straight ahead, so he could grab both of my ankles. With his face pushed into the clay, he turned his head and indicated that Mr. Haskins should throw some pitches. As the ball neared the plate, Mr. Mitchell lifted my front foot, moving it six inches toward the pitcher's mound. Over and over he did this until I learned the process of stepping into a pitch, of anticipating the ball's arrival by stepping toward it as it raced to the plate, of shifting my body weight to counteract the ball's momentum. It was a rather awkward lesson, for Mr. Mitchell at least, and it was unsuccessful. My lack of hand and eye coordination could not overcome whatever improvements in footwork he had brought about.

In the seventh grade, Mr. Ghelarducci gave extra batting practice on countless Saturdays, demanding that I hold the bat in different ways and at different angles. If I got on a hitting roll during a Saturday practice, though, it was inevitably gone by Sunday's game. He tucked me in the last spot in the batting order, at least proving Sherm's adage that there was always room on the team, and in this case on the field, for a kid who played good defense. I liked wearing the uniform and took pride in my defense. But I feared hitting, and the fear came close to taking the fun from the game.

In the summer before my eighth-grade year, though, my love for the game was fully restored.

My coach then in the San Bruno city league was Tom Lara, Jr. His father was the city's baseball don—he ran the show and coached the city's best teams. Short and squat, Senior occasionally smoked a thick cigar as he hit infield practice before games. He wore windbreakers always, even in the heat, and was a ubiquitous presence at diamond number one, the beautiful field with a grandstand in San Bruno Park.

His oldest son was a rebel. Tommy wore his long hair slicked back, and his chin usually bore several days growth. His car could be heard blocks away, and he generally pulled up just a few minutes after practice was to start, figuring his kids could warm up without him. He was loud and cussed in the presence of young boys. He often looked as if he had been through a lot, though at twelve I wasn't quite sure what that meant. I just knew that he looked much older than he was, and he was in his late twenties.

We were a miserable team, and I in particular was having a

miserable year hitting. I don't know if I had gotten a single hit halfway through the season, a nearly unbearable stretch. One day, Tommy asked me—told me, rather—to stay after practice so we could work on my hitting. Over the course of the next five days, he gave me more than three hours of his time. Me, alone with Tommy Lara, for an hour on three different days.

"We're gonna break this down, Sweeney," he said. "You're gonna hit the fuckin' ball. I'm gonna teach you, and you're gonna be a fuckin' hitter." At that point, I would not have believed those words from a single person, especially not him. I was more touched than excited.

Tommy Lara did break it down. Like a hungover dance teacher, he fumbled with the words and descriptions, turning away to cough every now and then, but was able to isolate each of the necessary body movements. He opened my stance dramatically. Instead of positioning me so that my body faced home plate and I looked at the pitcher over my left shoulder—the traditional batter's position—he turned my body so that I squarely faced the pitcher. He told me to choke way up on the bat, so that on a thirty-inch bat, only twenty inches of wood remained above my hands. I held the bat parallel to the ground, and as he pitched, I was to lift my left foot straight up and move it slightly toward the pitcher. He had me use barely half a swing, starting with the bat over the plate, prodding me to draw my face as close to the ball and bat as I could while making this abbreviated swing. He wanted my eyes wide open, watching cowhide hit wood from a distance of a foot or so. By cutting down on my movements, he created a process where I would essentially watch the ball reach my bat. By the end of the hour, I must have hit fifty balls in a row. None went past the pitcher's mound, but that wasn't the point.

"You're hittin' the fuckin' ball, Sweeney!" he shouted. "You're gonna be a fuckin' hitter!"

Two days later, at our next session, he moved my left foot a few inches, so that it was now pointing toward third base. When I stepped into the ball on this day, I was to move it more clearly toward the oncoming pitch. All of the action was right there in front of me; I was still facing the pitcher. My swing was now at three-quarters, and the hit balls did not go far—but I hit every pitch in or near the strike zone. On our third meeting, he again moved my front foot, so it was now pointed toward shortstop. The length and speed of my swing increased, but now he talked about using my wrists, snapping them quickly to punch the ball into a hole between the shortstop and third baseman, or delaying the snap to send the ball into a hole on the right side. I could control my bat speed by being aware of my wrists—when and how quickly they snapped.

In a week, I had gone from dreading every at bat, fearing every pitch, to deciding where I wanted to hit a pitched ball. I still couldn't hit it far, but I could hit a baseball.

Our next game was at windblown Lion's Field, and John Maxotoupolis had already mowed down eight San Bruno Merchants by the time I got to the plate in the third inning. He was a barrel-chested fireballer, and not a single one of my teammates had managed to hit a fair ball. As I stood in the box, my stance evoked the tiny Latin shortstops who played in the major leagues then; they were slap hitters with comical stances, but they controlled their bats well and made their living with speed and cunning. I had no speed, but I now had cunning. With my wooden Frank Robinson bat, I made contact with the very first pitch, a fastball. The ball shot toward the hole in the right side of the infield, where the second baseman made what I thought was a lucky grab of a ball skimming off its first hop. I was out at first but don't recall ever feeling more satisfied. I had hit a shot, and it took a good play to get me out.

Tommy Lara, standing in the coach's box at third base, didn't say a thing. He didn't say I had hit the fuckin' ball or that I was a fuckin' hitter. But he had a huge, closed-mouth smile and stared at me from the third-base coaching box as he clapped, loudly and deliberately, for a long, long time. He turned away, pulled his cigarettes from his back pocket, and lit up. He knew it and I knew it. I was a fuckin' hitter.

A few months later, in the fall of my eighth-grade year, the Fallons were visiting from southern California, and my uncle Bill came to watch my baseball game. He had seen me play before, when I couldn't hit a ball, and I was thrilled to have him in the stands now that I could. The city league was over now, and I wore the red-and-blue uniform of the St. Robert's Bears. Gary Herald, the pitcher for St. Veronica's, had a nasty curveball, particularly for an eighth grader, and my uncle talked to me about it before the game. "Go with the pitch," he said. "Step into it and hit it to the right side." It was advice I would not have understood before Tommy Lara's tutorial, but I kept it in mind.

Though I had been hitting the ball in practice, I had a history of ineptitude and was still batting last in this, our second game of the season. When I stepped to the plate, Greg Hart, the St. Veronica's catcher who would later be a good friend, shouted to the pitcher, "Number nine hitter, Gar. Number nine." It was utterly humiliating, public notice that I was the weakest hitter, an easy out for a pitcher like Gary Herald. Which, of course, I had always been. Gary threw a curveball that looked, as curveballs do, as if it was flying right toward my head. With my wide-open stance I could see everything—his hand, the ball, the field—and with my hands choked up on the bat, it felt like I was confidently wielding a simple tool, like a paring knife. The pitch would break to my right, I guessed, so I followed Uncle Bill's advice. I stepped toward the ball just when its trajectory changed. My body was moving right, the same direction the pitched ball was now moving. I was going with the pitch. I felt and heard the crack of the bat and slapped the ball on a soft line drive into right field. I stood there on first base, feeling the sting of Mr. Ghelarducci's congratulatory butt slap. It was all of ninety feet from home plate, but it was a long haul, and I had worked hard to get there. I went to second when the next batter walked, and scored on an error.

A few innings later, Greg again reminded Gary that I was

just the number nine hitter, this time saying aloud, "Easy out, Gar. Easy out." I stepped into a curveball and again hit it to right field. We lost five to two that day, but I could barely contain myself when my uncle and I walked into our house.

"Kevin's team got two hits today," he said before pausing. "And Kevin got both of them."

My uncle Bill had been there to see it, a fact that made an immense amount of difference to me. He knew the score, knew how many hits we had, knew why that spot near second base would open up. He knew what it meant to hit a curveball, what it meant to go with the pitch. And he saw me do it, all of it. I had always been a show-off, but this was different. This was about understanding, and Uncle Bill understood.

I batted second for the remainder of that season. I loved standing near home plate before games with Bobby Voreyer— the Voreyer brothers always batted leadoff—as we watched the opposing pitcher take his final warm-up throws. I was now a contact hitter, and if Bobby got on base, I knew the second baseman would run to cover the bag if Bobby tried to steal second during my at bat. That meant I could slap the ball right where the second baseman had been standing before he started running to meet the catcher's throw at second. It meant I could do what Sherm Heaney had talked about so often—hit behind the runner.

As a teenager in the city leagues, I hit third for my team and slowly developed the strength to hit the ball farther. I made the city all-star team. I hit a ball off the fence at Capuchino High School, on the same field where Wally Bunker had played.

That ball traveled more than three hundred feet, but I only ended up on second base; I could barely run because I couldn't believe I had hit a ball that far. I walked up to the plate relaxed, occasionally chatting with the umpire or opposing catcher.

Baseball is just a game, and hitting the ball is only part of the game. But those days with Tommy Lara were an important passage, one that feels, in hindsight, as if it made all other passages possible. It was important to me that I succeed at baseball, at least to a certain extent. It was important to me that my success did not come because I was gifted but because I had worked.

Tommy Lara wasn't the kind of coach parents liked, at least not then. He wasn't a model citizen and wasn't the kind of role model I was seeking. But during one week before my eighth-grade year, he gave me one of the great lessons a child can learn. It wasn't just that he taught me to hit a baseball. For that one week, I was the most important person in the world to him; I was his one project. His level of commitment led to magic. He taught me that we could break it down, that we could take a complex problem and figure it out, step by step. It's a process I've relied on since, and it's helped me greatly.

"We're gonna break this down, Sweeney," is what he said when he started the process. As we broke it down together, I was built up.

10

The Fatherless He Sustains

At the age of thirteen, I was confirmed as a "soldier of Christ." Confirmation comes along at an age when many religions sanction a passage to adulthood; the Catholic form is similar to most but generally involves fewer presents. In a regal ceremony, performed en masse, confirmees are blessed and anointed with oil by a bishop. He then gives each a ceremonial tap on the cheek, suggesting we would bear whatever suffering might be required to defend Christ's honor.

Part of the process of confirmation is the choosing of an extra name, a saint's name. This would be the name I would bear in the battle against sin, against Christ's enemies, against my own lack of will. Although that was how the literature framed it, the nuns at St. Robert's had already softened the hard edges of the Roman church's doctrine. It was not about fighting, they said; it was about adulthood. The extra name was not chosen to identify the saint whose sword we would bear in a vicious war against evil; it was a call for assistance in seeking out the good. A simple request, the calling of a name, so that someone might be there to help us make the tough decisions that came with our advancing years.

I took the process seriously. I liked the passage it represented, and the form the passage took. I would find a role model to help me. It was a process I knew well.

My sisters attempted to choose the names of saints who had been popular, pretty, or both, or so it seemed to my mother, who made each of them write a two-page essay on the saint's name they preferred. Aileen wanted Bridget but couldn't come up with enough words to justify the choice; she ended up with Catherine. I didn't need to write an essay when I told Mom the name I had chosen.

"Joseph," I said. "I want to be a good father, and he knew how."

I felt comfort in my plan to adopt the three fathers; by this point, unbeknownst to them, I had a store of references that I thought would serve me well. But I still wanted help. I still wondered. I didn't expect St. Joseph to help me—directly or indirectly—but saying his name aloud was a reminder to myself that I had more to learn, more gaps to fill.

———————

I didn't mind going to church then. Getting up on Sunday mornings was never a chore for me; I was an early riser. I liked seeing the Heaneys and other families afterward, talking for a few minutes as we stood outside the church doors. I liked the religious hymns, especially the ones with drama, like the "Gloria," or those that revealed unbearable sorrows, like the "Ave Maria" and all the other songs about Mary. I heard exactly what I was listening for in the mass: forgiveness. For six days a week, I felt judged, if not by the church, certainly by myself. I could be driven by guilt, by the gap between what the church demanded and how I lived. But at mass, on Sundays, I loved the English translation of the "Agnus Dei": Jesus, as the gentle Lamb, who would cleanse the world of its sin, of my sin. "Lord, I am not worthy to receive you," we said before communion, "but only say the word and I shall be healed." I was not worthy, not me, but only a word was required and the forgiving God would utter it. For me and for the others. I would be forgiven. I felt it right then—a feeling of liberation, of relief.

I was attentive in church when the readings turned to child rearing. Joseph was a faint shadow, barely visible in his son's light. A humble father, he knew the work was not about him, but about the child, Jesus. He was compassionate and forgiving, taking in Mary despite the embarrassment and anger that must have come in finding she was pregnant with a child not his own. He was a father figure, but not exactly a father. That made him more familiar to me, a boy with father figures but no father.

I remember a reading in which Jesus tells of the poor widow who gave a far greater share of her meager wealth than the richest men in Galilee, just as my mother did when the hat was passed. She would not say so directly, but it was a passage my mother hated, to have a woman boiled down and described simply for the absence of her husband. She squirmed in her seat when the priest, in no position to know, talked of the goodness of the widow. It was, she suggested later, a bit more complicated. I loved the passage.

There were references to children without fathers. "The Lord protects strangers, the widow and the fatherless he sustains." It was right there in the Psalms, the responsorial song early in the church year. I was not mentioned by name in Psalm 146, but the absence was mere coincidence—that was about me, about my sisters, about people like us. We were different. It is stunning to me now that I could find an excuse for arrogance in the Psalms, but I did. Us kids without dads, those of us who worked, were better than rich kids. The Psalms had given me permission.

The church was so much a part of who we were. The priests at our house for dinner. The rosaries at Grandma's. The joining of two dozen hands for grace before a Thanksgiving dinner at our cousins, the Deslers. Much of it was heavy, laden with fear and guilt. How could it not be, with its roots so deep in Ireland? Still, the nuns and younger priests at St. Robert's struggled to make it lighter for us, translating the mysterious Latin *gaudete* into its plain English counterpart: joy. The church was becoming approachable. The pastor then, an ancient Irish import, had no idea that the younger clerics he supervised during my final years in grammar school had embraced a sort of liberation theology. They were driven by service to the Lord but focused on the needs and rights of humanity. They didn't quite care if it came through prayer, corporal works of mercy, or outright political action. We had pen pals in Vietnam, we lit candles when

Dr. King was shot, we pushed for advances in the War on Poverty—all because our nuns raised the subjects.

My mother and her friends talked aloud of faith. Not often, and never to preach, it was most often done as an aside. "Sometimes you just need to put yourself in the Good Lord's hands," I remember hearing Dolores Kelly say. That was it, but it was clear that they trusted something, that they had faith.

I was not pious. Not by a long shot. I was still an altar boy, but by then only the title, cassock, and white lace smock hinted of an angelic child. As eighth graders, we were now top-of-the-rung boys and were given our pick of the best celebrations. Saturday weddings were good gigs, because the best man usually tipped, but funerals for the elderly indigent were at the top of our list. These poor souls had no known relatives to serve with the priests on their behalf, as my cousins and I did when Grandpa Sweeney was laid to rest. Because it would be an embarrassment, perhaps even sad beyond measure, to have a solitary priest stand alone before a small handful of survivors, two of us were plucked from the eighth-grade classroom to stand by. Sure it was a funeral, but it meant we were out of school for nearly two hours, and what could be better than that?

Pat Cilia and I were chosen for the task most often. His oldest brother was already in the seminary, studying to be a priest, and I was the red-haired son of a widow; we were a perfect pair to bear witness to a long life just expired. We left the classroom at twenty minutes to the hour, giving us time to roughhouse before dressing for the funeral mass. Walking down Oak Avenue, we knew our destiny for the remainder of the morning. Like moths before a flame, like a six-in-the-morning drunk down at Newell's on San Mateo Avenue, we didn't really have a choice at this point; our path had been cut. It was full of unspeakable dangers, and we loved it.

The mass commenced solemnly, as it would with a casket right there before us. We knelt on opposite sides of the altar, behind the priest and therefore out of his view, but fully visible to the congregation, however small it might be. Pat and I struggled mightily not to make eye contact, but inevitably it happened. He caught my eye, or I caught his. One of us smiled, and that was it. Never out loud but always on cue, we started to laugh. We were laughing at a funeral, and nothing on heaven or earth could stop us once we started. Our faces contorted and our shoulders shook. We looked at each other for an instant, then to the carpeted steps, tears now running down our cheeks. We spent the next half hour alternately biting our lips, holding our breath, or conjuring up any image, anything, that might stop us from laughing. We struggled to make it look as if we might be crying, or hoped the attendees were so old that they might not see us well enough to really know. It seemed we went minutes without breathing, then gasped for air before shifting into even deeper convulsions. We knelt all the while. One morning, I had to pull out my handkerchief and hold it over my nose, as if I was about to start a horrible sneezing spell, so I could walk off the altar and out the side door, where I let out a huge burst of air and laughter.

Amid all of this, if we could manage, we stole hosts from the sacristy. They were unconsecrated, and we put handfuls of them in our pockets, eating them during class, or gently placing one on a girl's outstretched tongue during recess. The girls said "amen" softly to us as they leaned back with open mouths. Right there on the playground at St. Robert's, it was a lush mixture of forbidden pleasures.

11

A Matter of When

Serra High School, named for Junipero Serra, the Spanish priest who established the chain of California missions, was an all-male Catholic school.

I chose to attend Serra, with my mom's blessing, because my brother had gone there, and so did the older boys from other families on our block—the Fanucchis, Garbans, and Ranneys. Two of Chick Kelly's sons—Neil and Tim—would also be there. And I chose it because there were no girls. I was tired of being in a house full of girls, but I was also afraid of them, and an all-boy school felt safer. With my mom working, Pat nearly finished with college, and Aileen having just moved out on her own, we had more money now, but the cost of a Serra High School tuition was still huge for us. I could attend Serra if I paid for half. It was $600 per year then, so my share was $300.

My mom favored Serra because she wanted me to continue with religious education, but also because she wanted me to find male influences. Unaware of my own strategy for finding them, she may have assumed that any Catholic man—or a whole mess of them—would do for the job of role modeling. What she didn't know is that it's hard to find good male role models in an all-male institution.

With nothing but boys in the student body and nothing but men on the faculty, there was nothing to temper the roiling masculinity. We couldn't be afraid, couldn't be open to the sensitive, couldn't be contemplative. We laughed at anything that might stop or slow what felt like a natural momentum toward destructiveness. It was a loud and wild place, and if silence reigned during class time, the school was merely a filling balloon waiting to be popped.

Every activity was shaped by, and ultimately consumed by, the need to determine a pecking order, to establish the alpha males. This recollection may be misleading—there may well have been boys undistracted by the competition, but if there were, I didn't notice them. I don't know why I needed to be alpha, and for a long time—even back then, when it was happening—I wondered about the possible voids, the longings, that might cause me to go to such absurd lengths, to be so needy for attention and respect. My new friend Dan Keefe and I would talk about it. *Why do we do this stuff? It's so senseless.* Our questions were serious, though we asked them in sarcastic tones, and then went on to do more of the same. I could not accept at the time that it might simply be who I was, who we were. In a pool of only males, my nature required that I attempt to be an alpha of some kind. I couldn't help it. Of course, neither could eight hundred other boys, which made the school both scary and exciting.

Teachers were often distracted, spending much of their time stifling male competitions or engaging in them directly. The best teachers simply went with the flow.

Typing class offered proof that boys could compete over anything. Typing was a mandatory class for all freshmen—there was no getting out of it. We could not admit that it was a challenge—it was women's work, after all. Saying it was stupid had no value—everyone already knew it was stupid, and saying the obvious didn't help one climb the alpha ladder. What happened in my typing class, with the teacher's knowing acquiescence, was the same thing that unfolded in all typing classes at Serra: It evolved into a brutal, competitive struggle. We cheered friends on during tests, placing bets on who might win the race to forty words per minute. We mocked the posted goals by taking them extra seriously, by performing our work as if nothing in the world was more important—nothing—than typing sixty words a minute. The boys in the first row of desks faced off against the second row, the third row faced off against the fourth, with the winners going head-to-head in a Friday type-off. The best among us would give a wide-eyed stare at friends while typing—proving we didn't need to look at the keys. By the end of the semester, many of the boys were typing forty words per minute or more, with very few mistakes. We had become typing badasses.

I was the only freshman in a sophomore English class, and I loved the opportunity to show up older boys. This was not about love of literature, it was about gambling on tests. Mr. Schaeffer, our teacher, joined in, offering a double-or-nothing challenge on a test. If you took the challenge and gained a perfect score, your point total was doubled; if one or more of your answers were wrong, you received a failing grade. I taunted the others when I discovered I was the only one to take the challenge, but they followed Neil Kelly's lead and loudly cheered on my behalf when I aced the test, slapping my back and chanting my name. I don't know what Mr. Schaeffer would have actually done if I had erred. He talked with us about English skills that could offer access to ideas or riches; we talked about kicking ass.

I could never really kick ass, of course, if kicking ass meant winning a fistfight. I was skinny and goofy and had no interest whatsoever in hitting or getting hit. Dan Keefe could physically challenge people then but was too smart to bother with fighting. The two of us were the alpha humorists, though, and once we established our dominance, we constantly took risks to defend it.

It was expected of us, and we needed to be funny on demand. We could do this, largely because our desire to make others laugh became an obsession. We could look spontaneous because we were often prepared—we had routines, or key elements of what would become a routine, down pat. We often played the role of Robin Hood, defending those persecuted by the school's toughs—there were in fact boys who could and did cause genuine physical harm. We could make fun of the toughs, in their presence, partly because Rick Garban (we no longer called him Ricky) was an excellent football player and was my friend. Mostly we could do it because our jokes then were funny and on target, and beating the crap out of us would have shown the bigger kids to be overly sensitive to insult. Hitting us would have proved their vulnerability.

Amid all the noise, it was still clear that there were many good kids at Serra, a fact that the competitions could neither hide nor alter. Most of the battles were lighthearted, and the observers were quite often supportive—if a fellow student wasn't engaged in the competition, he could at least acknowledge that being on the spot was tough. It was a bit like being in a big family; we all knew we were being tested in the same way, and we used it to form camaraderie. I liked the bigger school, with a gene pool filled with its share of smart kids. I liked going to school with one of my cousins, Kevin Desler. And I liked that I now was in school with two of the Kelly boys; family relations trumped the usual high school boundaries set by age, and the Kelly boys and I got on well, though they were both ahead of me in years.

It was all in good fun at Serra. If you pulled decent grades and didn't get too caught up in the roughhousing, what was there to fear?

We drank at Serra, or at least my friends and I did. We drank a lot.

My friends at St. Robert's had older siblings who drank, as did some of mine, giving us a sense that it was just what kids did. We neither decided to be kids who drank, nor did we consider being kids who didn't. Kids like us drank. It was simply another field of play, another way to join a club, another way to fit in. If bridge had been the tradition, perhaps we would have arranged pairs and foursomes. I don't recall many parents asking about alcohol back then; if it came up at all, it was admonition to avoid drink, or to at least not get drunk.

We started after eighth grade, at the park on the way to our first co-ed party. We drank enough to get a taste, enough to realize that a taste for alcohol would need to be acquired. Though we hadn't had enough to feel it, we certainly had enough to get a story out of it, to boast, to put ourselves in position to exaggerate, which we did. We also drank enough to inextricably link, at least for a while, these two new tastes—girls and alcohol. There we were in the park, skinny thirteen-year-old boys, still years away from shaving, our voices not yet changed. And we were drinking.

At Serra, our drink was beer, purchased by older siblings, or by one of the strangers we approached in the shadows outside liquor stores—we asked them to "buy up" for us.

We drank before and after our school's varsity football and basketball games. These were night games, usually against all-male schools, and often in the big city, San Francisco, a drive of half an hour or more. With both sets of stands well oiled, fights broke out often on the way to and from.

We drank at parties, held most often at the homes of kids whose parents were away. Each boy carried his own badge of honor, a six-pack wrapped in a brown paper bag, tucked securely under his arm. Houses could be trashed in an instant. All is well one moment, and a fight breaks out the next. Drinks are spilled, a window is broken, and the crowd takes off before or when the cops arrive. Most of the kids were well behaved—if one can accept that young kids consuming alcohol might be polite and well behaved—but, well, it only takes a few. I cringed for the hosts of a party, feeling sorry for them in advance of the inevitable. But I still showed up; Keefe and I both did. We sipped our beer and held court in the kitchen, backyard patio, or wherever else we could find a crowd. Our audience would grow as our jokes grew louder and more ambitious.

We drank before, during, and after the Catholic teen club dances we attended at least once a month. These were social events at which a local parish hosted a nighttime dance for its teens, opening the doors to kids from the entire peninsula. The good Catholic families sent their sons to all-boy schools and their daughters to all-girl schools, so this was the chance to meet Catholics of the opposite sex, to develop social skills under adult supervision. But the lights were low, and any adult chaperones were overwhelmed by ten o'clock. Who knew what went on? I sure didn't.

Drinking at games was a result of peer pressure, something that might have been obvious if I had stopped to think about it. Drinking at dances was different, though, and I fully understood my reasons for doing so. I was petrified. I had no problems meeting girls at dances or parties. I could meet anyone; Keefe and I both could. I could walk up to the prettiest girl at a party, introduce myself, and entertain her—and all of her friends—for an hour in the kitchen. But I could not ask for her phone number. I could not ask her to dance. As a little boy, I could not express my sadness; as a big boy, I could not profess my love. If I could never say I was jealous, how could I say I desperately wanted something, or someone? I couldn't recognize the connections then, that the suppression of one emotion might lead to the suppression of another; I just knew I could not find the words I needed. I also feared a girl's rejection more than anything in the world, and I assumed the rejections would flow: I had red hair and freckles, was skinny and physically awkward, and could not imagine a pretty girl liking me.

No one would know of these fears and restraints. I masked them perfectly with humor, so much so that nearly everything I had was invested in laughter. But I could not find ways to transform this humor into an expression of affection.

And so I drank in the hopes that I might find courage. I drank to distract me from my assumed fate. After a while, I don't know, I just drank.

During my freshman year, Maureen Curran married. She was a distant cousin and the first of my generation to marry. Her father was Red Curran, said to be one of our daddy's favorites. How they culled one from the many to be given the name "Red" was always a mystery to me, if not an outright joke. "He's the one with red hair" was more a punch line at a Sweeney gathering than a navigational guide.

The wedding was at a Catholic high school in San Jose, some forty miles from our house. We loved the chance to visit with cousins, aunts, and uncles—even in our teens, the luster of these visits never paled. Our aunts, in particular, were stunning in their love for us, and a five-minute chat with each was worth the drive. We adored them and loved that they adored us.

Uncle Roger wore a green suit that day, nearly upstaging the bride, and a few of the men were well on their way to drunk not long into the party. I danced with my sisters and aunts and prepared for the obligatory dance with Mom. Anne pulled me aside in the middle of a conversation with cousins.

"Get your coat and meet us at the car," she whispered. "We're leaving, but we can't say good-bye. Do not say good-bye to anyone."

The toasts had not been given, the cake had not been cut, and Red hadn't yet cried while trying to speak of his family's love, as we knew he would. Leaving without thanking the hosts was unconscionable, but we were leaving.

I knew from Anne's face that something was horribly wrong, and as I walked from the building, I saw it.

Terry and Aileen emerged from the bathroom, quickly moving to the door as they shielded our mother, who was sobbing. They ushered her into the car, where she sat in the front seat, between her two oldest daughters. Our mother sobbed deeply, uncontrollably, endlessly. It was the most heartbreaking sound I had ever heard—for the entire forty-five minute drive, my mother cried. She wailed. None of us kids spoke, none of us could speak. The only sounds were the hum of the freeway and our mother's heaving sobs. Over the course of the drive, I fought back tears of my own.

It was the warmth and the music and the dancing that had hit Mom so hard. She was so happy, so full of her happiness, so aware of it all. And then it hit her, in the dancing, that the dancer with whom she had shared so much could not share this day. They could not share this day or any day. In an instant, she missed her husband terribly—right then and there and all the way home. She missed him because she was happy, and that was the hardest hit of all, that the sadness would rise up at the height of her happiness. Then she missed him even more because he could not comfort her sadness.

My mother's sobs were a genuine shock to me. I had never seen her cry so hard for so long, nor had I ever seen her cry tears that were unmasked by any other emotion. These could not be interpreted as tears of frustration or anger or fatigue; these were tears of sadness. Daddy had been dead ten years and my mother was not yet over the loss. It was as if she had just been told; that's how raw she was.

By the time we crested the hill on Cypress Avenue, my interpretation of what was happening was complete. I now understood that the pain associated with the loss of a loved one was both deep and lasting. It could be unfathomably deep. I thought then that I had seen suffering, real suffering, for the first time in my life. I thought I was coming to an understanding of the sadness in the world. And I thought, on that day and not necessarily by choice, that I was no longer a boy, but a man. I had seen the world in its true harshness. I had seen my mother in such obvious need. My time as a man had arrived.

The irony of this understanding was lost on me. I, too, had lost a loved one, but I could not recognize the pain of such a loss until I saw it in someone else.

During these first two years of high school, I saw Chick Kelly fairly often. He still dropped by on occasion to check in on our mother, and I could always join in for part of those visits. I saw him when friends and I stopped in to pick up Neil on the way to a game or a party. I also saw him at events at Serra. At afternoon games, when there was no drinking, we might have a fairly long visit; at night games, if I had beer in me, I kept the conversation brief. I didn't seek him out deliberately at games but always enjoyed seeing him when I did.

The Kelly kids staged a twenty-fifth wedding anniversary for their parents. A surprise party, it began in church with a mass. The kids had figured their parents, married in a church, would want to remember it in a church as well. And so Chick and Dolores, twenty-five years into their marriage, stood before the congregation and happily exchanged their vows again. We all moved to the parish hall afterward for a reception, the Sweeney kids stepping in to help serve the potluck dinner. They were a wonderful couple, obviously in love. Chick was gracious to his wife, and a good dancer.

During my sophomore year, I saw Chick often because I played football on the junior varsity with Neil Kelly. Dan Keefe was also on the team. I played because it was Serra High, and Serra was a football school. I really could find no other reason for playing beyond my desire to fit in. The sport wasn't for me, and when I wasn't bored, I was bemused.

Before our games, Coach Carboni gathered his young Catholic charges together in prayer.

"All right, all right, all right," he would say every Saturday. "Come on in, come on in, men. Put your hands in here." We formed a circle around the coach, each boy with an arm extended toward the center, and he asked us to pray that no one would get hurt. In the same cadence and volume he used to call plays or shout instructions, he yelled out the first half of the Hail Mary. As if on command, we all followed suit by shouting the second half of the prayer. Sixty boys in shoulder pads and helmets, shouting the Hail Mary as loudly as they could. As soon as the verse was finished, Mr. Carboni screamed out, "Our Lady, Queen of Victory!" I had never before heard the Blessed Virgin Mary described in such a way.

"Pray for us!" we shouted.

And then he yelled what we all waited for. "Let's go to war!"

Boys now screamed at the top of their lungs, shouting nothing and everything. Only seconds away from the Hail Mary, we spoke of war and put together unspeakable combinations of cusswords. Boys jumped on each other, banged helmets, slammed fists into each other's shoulder pads. Keefe and I looked at each other like we had somehow found ourselves stuck in the middle of a nuthouse, which in fact was the case. He slammed my shoulder pads, I pushed him in the chest, and we both walked away down the sidelines, shaking our heads. Keefe actually played; I did not.

I knew, a mere two days into our practices, that I did not like tackle football. I not only didn't like getting tackled, I didn't even like tackling others. For three full months, I lived with the knowledge that if I had any guts or integrity I would quit. But I could not bring myself to quit, out of fear of being labeled a *pussy,* Serra High's worst insult. Quitting football was far worse than not going out in the first place, an option that at least allowed one to claim indifference to the sport.

Had we won our last game that season, we would have shared the league's championship, and I hoped a championship might make it all worth it. But we lost that game, 12–0. The Kelly men were all along the sidelines that day. Chick, his two sons-in-law, his two oldest boys—they were all there as one to watch Neil playing the game they all loved. Neil had an unabashed love of football and, in particular, a love of hitting; when he played against a cousin who attended a different school, the two of them kept hitting each other, smiles on their faces, long after the whistle blew. The Kellys were born to it, and I wasn't. It was the only time I felt estranged from them, like I didn't belong, or couldn't belong, to the same clan.

I went into the locker room with tears in my eyes after that last game. I wasn't crying because of the defeat; I was disgusted with myself. A real man would have quit this nonsense long ago.

Toward the end of my sophomore year, I started to lose control.

Although I had been drinking for some time, now I was drinking more. More often and in greater quantities. I was drunk once a week, certainly, and sometimes more. There was a day when I drank at school, in the cafeteria. I didn't drink there because I craved alcohol, but because I craved attention. But after a while, after enough alcohol, what difference would it make?

For the first time, I got sick from alcohol, throwing up everything I had taken in during the previous week—solid or liquid—or so it seemed. I got sick a few weeks later as well. I was embarrassed by the loss of control but could still joke about it, could still laugh it off in the presence of others. When alone, though, I could be consumed with self-hatred. How could I be so stupid? Why do I drink like that?

There was a stretch of four consecutive weekends that spring when I arrived home much later than the curfew my mom had imposed. If she said I was to be home by midnight, I would stay out until 1:00 or 2:00. I didn't call her in advance to say I was going to be late; I just got home when I got home. I didn't do this with malice or even intent; I just couldn't force myself to leave a party before others did. I felt bad about my behavior, but I ignored Mom's rules. I ignored her.

Until Chick Kelly stepped in.

We were at their house on a weekend night. It was not a big visit; only a few kids from each family were around. After the table had been cleared and the dishes done, Chick suggested that he and I talk for a few minutes. I was now as tall as he was, more than six feet; we could stand together and look each other in the eye, but on this night, he led me to the end of their dining room table, where we both sat. My mom and Dolores were talking quietly in the living room; all the others were out of sight. I could tell that this was about something awkward, perhaps even troubling.

His voice was strong and soothing, but it was also clear that what he was saying was not easy for him. He fumbled through a few sentences about how powerful alcohol could be, how dangerous it could be, and I now knew the topic. I had known for some time that my mother was troubled by my behavior; now someone else was. Chick clearly knew at least as much as she did, and probably more. Perhaps my mom had raised it with him; perhaps one of his sons had given him the details. He didn't say I had been drinking—he didn't accuse me of anything—but my drinking was silently acknowledged by both of us.

Chick cut to the chase.

"The way you're acting is hurting your mother, and I won't tolerate that," he said.

I felt stricken and must have looked it. I couldn't say anything in response, but nodded my head, as if to say "yes." After a long silence, he changed his tone.

"I don't think you're becoming the man you want to be," he said. "You're not on the way to becoming the man I know you can be."

He said that he knew there was something in me, something special. He said I had shown him I had the potential to be a good man. I wasn't on the right path just then, he said, but he had faith that I soon would be. He told me he knew I would make better choices. He knew I would.

"I know you'll make better choices," he said. "It's simply a matter of when."

I was astonished. He was both strong and loving, an obvious combination, but not one I had noticed before. He had shown faith in me. He wasn't trying to slap me down or stamp me out, but sought to unleash the good that was right there in me. A topic that always gravitated toward self-hatred had been reshaped. He was telling me not to be so hard on myself—but to start being smart. I knew I didn't want to disappoint my mother, but Chick reminded me that I didn't want to disappoint myself. I had choices. A man had choices. This is what I inferred, then and later, from the conversation.

For so many years, I had hung on his every word. I had watched him with his sons, with his wife, with my mother. Now, I was no longer mere observer; I was the subject. I had always been aware of a detachment between my chosen fathers and me, but now the distance was gone. I was engaged in a father-son chat with a father I had chosen.

I barely said a word in response; there was little I could say. I was overwhelmed, inspired, and relieved. Chick moved on to talk about other things, and, moments later, we were interrupted.

His words had weight. The one conversation did not turn me around, did not wean me completely from alcohol. But it set me on a different path. I can still see Chick Kelly's table, the spot of the only real father-son chat I would ever have, perhaps the only one I would ever need. It was enough. It was enough to feel accepted, to feel loved. It was enough to help me make different decisions, to think more about what it was that I wanted to be. It was enough to learn how, to feel as if I would know what to say if and when I myself became a father.

I left Serra after my sophomore year and enrolled in Crestmoor High School, the local public school. I had paid for half of the tuition during each of my first two years, but both the tuition and my share would increase for the final two years. I had good friends at Serra, great friends, but the obvious conclusion was that it wasn't worth the money. Not for me, at least. I needed to start saving for college.

Although the decision was mostly about money, I realized as well that moving on, altering bad habits, might be easier with a change of scenery.

Choosing to transfer schools was a difficult process, particularly for a boy not yet sixteen. But I made the decision on my own and did so feeling certain I had done the right thing. What I didn't see then was that I was being passed from the hands of one chosen father into the hands of another.

12

Showing Up

The Bacigalupi family may have seen a blank canvas when I interviewed for a job at La Dora, the delicatessen they owned and named for the family's matriarch. They may have felt comfortable with me, having seen me walk in there occasionally with Grandma Fallon, who lived just down the street from the deli. Or they may have noticed an uncommon passion for Italian salami as we sat down over sandwiches in the back room during my interview. Whatever the reason, they hired me. I now had the best job a fifteen-year-old could possibly find in San Bruno.

The pay was great. Working twenty hours a week during the school year, I made more in one month than I would in five months of delivering newspapers. I had loved the feeling of independence I gained at ten when I had my own consistent source of spending money, but now it was real money, in quantities that gave me genuine choices. I didn't need to spend money on a car or gas—the deli was a five-minute bike ride from our house— so I could salt away a large amount of money every month, and did so. Saving for college on a weekly and monthly basis made it a reality for me—it was proof that I would indeed apply for, and enroll in, a four-year college. That had never been a foregone conclusion for me or anyone else in our family; a college degree was not an assumed right or a perceived requirement for success. It had not been described as a measure, really, of anything. I had assumed I would go to college, largely because my own ego and ambitions required it—I was planning to be active in politics— but I hadn't thought much about what it really meant, what it would require, both in terms of grades or money. Now that I was on track financially, working to improve my grades (which had suffered at Serra) seemed an easier task, even if this new job required that I work until eleven o'clock some weeknights. I was no longer working simply for pocket change or to catch up with the other kids; I was working toward something, working to be something.

I loved the food. Before my tenure at La Dora, I had tasted only the blandest of processed cheeses: Swiss, American, cheddar. We did have Parmesan cheese from a can, but for my entire childhood, we pronounced it "par-MEE-see-an." Now I held court over a deli counter with more than seventy varieties of cheese at any one time. Paul Bacigalupi, Dora's son, insisted that I taste and know each variety, asking me to describe the flavor of the cheeses he and I might be wrapping just then. *Can you taste the smoky flavor of the imported Edam? Compare the richness of these two Brie wheels.* I tasted lox for the first time, and Paul taught me to slice it so the filet had a neat, straight cut. I tasted all of the Italian and German meats and learned to place waxed paper between the thin, thin slices of prosciutto. I knew the different brands of Italian salami by their color, taste, and smell—it was no longer just salami—and I could discern the maker of a San Francisco sourdough roll by touch or by taste. I had a sandwich of my choice on each shift and could buy meats to bring home for half price. When I brought home salami for my mother, it was actually a pile and it was all for her. Chick Kelly still brought the steaks; now I brought the deli meats.

Paul was exceptionally polite and doted on customers, particularly women. He found a million ways to prolong a conversation with a woman, walking round the counter to stand next to her as she picked out the cheeses for the weekend feast. The deli staff then was mostly high school boys, and we learned from Paul's people skills—though we applied them with more humor. We flirted endlessly with female customers, regardless of their age. If a pretty woman in her thirties wanted to purchase wine, we asked for her ID; once, after I had done so, a woman leaned across the counter, grabbed my face in her hands, and planted a quick kiss on my lips. If a female classmate was in with her mother, we asked if her *sister* wanted anything, feigning surprise when we learned it was actually her mother. We made Grandma's friends laugh when we greeted them with a "Can I help you, *young lady?*"

Paul was a fanatic for good-quality service, and on days when he could not inspire it out of us, he demanded it. There was no legitimate reason, ever, for doing anything less than top-quality work. If we were to clean the counter surfaces, why would we even consider doing a less-than-perfect job? If we were to wrap the deli meats in white butcher paper, why would we not arrange the meats neatly and set crisp corners on the package as we folded and taped it shut? It should all be done quickly. We were to look customers in the eye when addressing them.

The lawns I had mowed for years were always neat when I finished a job; my brother had shown me how to do that. But when working at close quarters, I simply did not know how to be neat. My desks, backpacks, and homework all were sloppy— always. Paul showed me that, when necessary, I could do crisp and perfect work as well as anyone. He taught me this because, at his deli, it was an absolute necessity.

I loved working for him and learning from him; he was a boss I deeply respected.

The Bacigalupis sold the deli a year after I was hired, and the new owners decided each employee could only play one after-school sport per year. They had grown tired of juggling our schedules in season. It was the middle of basketball season when they announced the policy, and I was playing on the varsity; quitting the team seemed out of the question. Quitting the deli was also not a consideration; it was my best ticket to college. Without much deliberation, I dropped baseball. Had I thought much about it, I would have been heartbroken, as I was years later when I actually did think about the decision. But under the circumstances, at the time, it was an easy choice. It was work, but it was often fun and rarely a burden; I was grateful to have the job.

At my new school, Crestmoor High, Sherm Heaney's son Dennis and I played basketball together.

Our team manager was an autistic boy, Kirk, who would crouch down low to the floor near the end of our bench. When the Crestmoor Falcons scored a bucket, he would leap high into the air, his arms and legs spread-eagled. When he landed, often awkwardly, he crouched down again in an instant. In that position, he rocked back and forth, back and forth, repeating the score and outlining the mathematical possibilities that lay ahead.

"Fifty-four to forty-eight, we're behind. Fifty-four to forty-eight, we're behind. Three more baskets, we tie. Three more baskets, we tie. Two baskets and two free throws and we tie. One basket, four free throws we tie. Six free throws, we tie. Four baskets, we lead by two." It was an endless mumbling, but if one wasn't annoyed by the banter, it was hard not to notice that his message was always a hopeful one. It was never over, not with Kirk. We might still win. Really, we might. When a player was replaced during a game, or when the team came together for a time-out, Kirk frantically handed out towels and water, then offered a steady and relentless clapping to encourage his mates.

I was not an aggressive competitor then. I practiced often, shooting baskets in front of our house or playing in pickup games at the San Bruno Rec Center. The Rec Center was where the NBA's Warriors had practiced when the team was still based in San Francisco, and it remained a preferred court for professional or major college basketball players who spent their summers on the peninsula. The competition was intense, but I wasn't. Others worked at their games—they worked hard to improve their skills—but I simply played.

After Saturday morning practices at the high school, four of us—Dennis Heaney, Larry Navilhon, Don Gillman, and I—would stop at the local 7-Eleven to buy Slurpees. Four of us boys, all too big for the tiny car, and we waited until everyone had piled in before taking our first sips. We each drew in deeply through the straws, and seconds later felt the crushing brain-freeze headache that comes from drinking an iced drink quickly. "Aauuggghhh!" We all screamed aloud for the ten seconds or so that it took for the headache to pass, and then we got on with our Slurpees and our Saturday morning. Ritual, it turned out, was an important part of our lives.

The next stop, for Dennis and me, was often his house. By this time, Sherm might have already played a round of eighteen holes. He golfed every Saturday morning, calling in at six o'clock to get the first available tee time; if he got it, he might even be home by the time the kids were up and about, and that was important to Sherm. Lunch in the Heaneys' kitchen was usually with both parents, who chatted with us as if they were one of our gang—or as if we were one of theirs. We talked about what had happened at practice; both Sherm and Dee were intensely interested in the coach's techniques, though they rarely offered criticisms—even when their disagreement with the approach was obvious.

I still loved watching games on television with Sherm. On Saturdays, it was college football; on Sundays, it might be professional basketball. His wasn't a constant banter—he could go long stretches without joining in on the conversation. But he always seemed to comment on an elegant play, a smart pass, or excellent teamwork.

A high school basketball season can be cluttered with two dozen or more games, often played at odd times. A holiday tournament might give us three games in three days, and weekday games were usually played right after school, before most of the working parents might be home from work. No matter where or when we played, Sherm was there. For afternoon games, he showed up in his suit, a car full of work no doubt awaiting the game's end. He might be a few minutes late, but he would be there ultimately.

When Sherm spoke up from the stands, it was only as encouragement. He would speak at a point when the crowd was quiet enough—a few seconds or so after the play was made—so the player involved might actually hear the compliment or encouragement. "Nice pass, Denny," he'd say to his son, as a time-out was called. "Nice screen, Kev," he'd say to me a few moments after a teammate had scored. Sherm noticed the fundamentals. He encouraged Dennis to take his shots, but it was the screens, assists, and rebounds that made his heart soar.

After games, a small handful of parents and friends would mill about in the foyer outside the locker room. Sherm was always one of them; he was always there. He had questions and comments for Dennis. And he had a question and a comment for me. Something specific, something unique about the game and my relation to it. He asked me, directly, about a particular play. If he noticed things we did wrong, he brought it up by pointing out things we "might want to work on before the next game," addressing failure by focusing on potential. A few tips and we parted ways, he and Dee going home, while Dennis and I and our friends went to wherever the night's meeting point was. I walked out of locker rooms all across San Francisco and San Mateo County, and there was always a dad there, ready to ask me questions and talk to me about the game. The cumulative impact of his steady presence was powerful, and it took on the same level of importance as my father-son chat with Chick Kelly. One of my chosen fathers was always there. If Sherm had failed to show at a game just once, I would have missed him.

Sherm was not the only person I noticed in the stands; quite often, he and Dee sat with my mother. And there were games when my brother, Pat, and his good friend Dennis O'Rourke would be in the crowd. They were grown men now, living in a house they had just purchased in San Bruno. At occasional afternoon or evening games, one or both of them would show up, Dennis still in his business suit or Pat in his uniform as a San Bruno firefighter. I noticed when they walked in, though I rarely acknowledged their presence during a game. I had watched the fathers watching their sons, and now Pat and Dennis were there watching me. It meant a great deal that they were there for me, for me alone.

I did not stop drinking when I attended Crestmoor, but I drank far less. There were many reasons for this shift, though I was likely unaware of many of them at the time. Chick Kelly's conversation had a lasting impact; he helped me see that the small decisions I made on a daily basis were adding up to be big decisions. My job at the deli made my path to college much more clear, and I had a sense that I was going somewhere. I fell into a circle of new friends, most of whom had enough self-confidence that they didn't see a need to rely on alcohol. I ended up with several very distinct sets of friends. These different groups all got along when they met up with one another, though they rarely blended. I was able to stay close to friends from Serra, and those relationships evolved as well; it was now easier to attend a party and not drink, or at least not get drunk. Some of the reasons were very straightforward and obvious, even then: My basketball coach, Pete Pontacq, insisted that any alcohol use whatsoever would lead to expulsion from the team, and that was a risk I was unwilling to take. And a good friend from the San Bruno Merchants baseball team, Ricky Smetzer, died while driving drunk.

This is not to say I didn't raise hell. With one group of friends, I pulled a long string of "runners" at restaurants, leaving the table and building without paying the bill. I insisted on being the last person out each time, not trusting my friends to get the job done right, and got away with the theft of food and service nearly a dozen times. Once, I was chased in a parking lot by a cook wielding a massive chopping knife; it would be the last runner I pulled. With another group of friends, I snuck into countless movie theaters without paying. Dennis Heaney and I saw *One Flew Over the Cuckoo's Nest* at least five times for free and had much of the movie memorized. My friends from Serra and I concocted elaborate schemes to sneak into Candlestick Park for Giants games, often overwhelming security guards with our numbers.

During my senior year, I was out late at a local pizzeria. A friend grabbed the remains of a pitcher of beer other customers had left behind. As he brought it to our table and poured rounds for boys still four years shy of the legal drinking age, a customer with a thick Italian accent started complaining. Shouting at us at close range, it sounded as if he wanted us to put the pitcher back, leave the restaurant, and who knows what else. We chose to leave—it was late, and I wanted to get home. He followed us to the parking lot, continuing to shout as we piled into our car. One of my friends said something to him before getting in—I wasn't quite sure what it was—and the man jumped in his car and raced down the street at what looked like seventy miles an hour. We kept pace for a few blocks, not quite knowing why, and then slowed down. We were a mile from my house, the night was over, and besides, we were about to pass the police station.

As we turned up Cypress Avenue, less than two hundred yards from my house, police lights went on everywhere. Flashing lights behind us and in front of us. Cops had pulled up from both directions to trap us. Bright white klieg lights shined in our car, making it nearly impossible to look up into the brightness. Using the shadow cast by the rearview mirror, I was able to make out one clear image: a cop, bent down on one knee, hiding behind an open squad car door, pointing a shotgun right at me. In the muffled tone of a police loudspeaker—the kind I had heard a thousand times on *Adam-12, Hawaii Five-0,* and other television shows—a cop walked us through our instructions.

"Make no sudden moves," said the voice over the loudspeaker. "Let me repeat that. No one is to make any sudden moves. Lift your hands up, very slowly, and place them on top of your heads. Very slowly." I had no idea why we had been pulled over, none of us did.

"Now, driver, I want you to slowly reach over with your left hand and remove the keys from the ignition. Your left hand, driver, your left hand. Good. Now slowly open the door, reach out, and drop the keys on the ground."

One by one, we followed the cop's instructions until all six of us were facedown on the pavement, spread-eagled, and being frisked. Midnight on Cypress Avenue, with four squad cars, four cops, a lot of weapons—and suspects lying on the ground. I kept imagining Mrs. Saisi walking out in her robe to say, "My gosh, isn't that Kevin there? Hey, Kevin! Hey!" But no one came out.

After searching the car, the cops found what they were looking for in the glove box. It was, in their words, "the plastic revolver." One of my friends had held a cap gun earlier in the evening and had it in his hand when he tossed an insult at the Italian. He didn't even notice that the gun—or what looked like a gun—was in his hand.

As the cops asked for our identification, I recognized one of them. He looked at my license, looked at me and asked, "Are you Aileen's brother?"

"I am, sir. I'm a Sweeney." I called him sir, even though he was only seven years older than me and had once dated my sister Aileen.

"You live about three houses from here, don't you?" he asked. When I corrected him and said it was closer to a dozen, he shook his head and said, "Go home."

That was it. I had been in cars pulled over by cops half a dozen times. I had worked my way through interviews illuminated by little more than a flashlight or the flashing lights of a squad car. But this was different. I knew we would instantly get a good story out of it—it was the talk of Crestmoor High for days—but I couldn't help thinking about my luck. What if we had moved suddenly? What if I hadn't known the cop? What if it had happened in the city or somewhere else where cops actually fire their guns? What if I had been caught on one of those many nights when I had actually broken the law? I hadn't done a thing wrong all evening—I hadn't sipped a drink, I wasn't driving and therefore was not speeding, I hadn't come close to breaking the law. But the randomness of it, the fact that a shotgun was pointed at my head, was a reminder that there were so many things I could not control—which in turn was a reminder to control the things I could.

If my mom knew what had happened that night, she didn't say anything. Not then, at least. When I mentioned it several years later, it was clear she had known the story's essential points, and she asked questions only to fill out her mental image of what had happened.

The family car was mine to use whenever I wanted, which was often, and I spent a great deal of time at Dan Keefe's house.

The Keefes were different from the Sweeneys. Dan's father was an eye surgeon, and his mother became an artist after spending years raising kids. They valued ideas, creative expression, and accomplishment. They were intellectuals and conversed on an utterly different plane than we did on Cypress Avenue. A person's decency mattered to the Keefes, but they swooned over a well-constructed argument. And if the construction wasn't elegant, they substituted volume. They shouted in their house, an unthinkable display of emotion in our family, and their arguments were both intense and full of humor.

Dan's father—I always addressed him as Dr. Keefe—was the quietest Keefe. He took in the arguments attentively, showing great pleasure as he watched and listened, but always seemed above it all. Not quite taciturn, he was steady and reserved. He was the only one in the household who never had to raise his voice to be heard.

The Keefes were wealthy and served as a foil while I explored my condescension toward the rich. If I held direct jealousies, they were couched in humor at the Keefes—partly out of habit and partly because humor was a requirement there. When we talked of class issues, the discussions started and ended easily because Dan had grown increasingly awkward about his family's wealth at roughly the same pace that I had grown confused by my own family's lack of it. Though the Keefe kids held jobs for at least part of each year, they showed great respect for the ways in which I worked to provide for myself. They respected me for how hard I worked and for my attitude about work, almost attaching greater value to my possessions or accomplishments than to their own. If I milked this by talking of the moral high ground the impoverished might occupy or began to exploit my fatherless status in an argument—something I did more than once—the Keefes would call me on it, gleefully.

They were ambivalent about basic family traditions, embracing them occasionally, ignoring them more often than not. One year their Christmas tree stood undecorated in the living room for two full weeks. Because they lived in a tony suburb, Dan and I chose to decorate in a way we thought would be culturally appropriate: We decorated the entire tree with one dollar bills. The Keefes thought it was hysterical and left it as is, opening their gifts in front of the one tree that expressed the true meaning of an American Christmas. They had several family photos in their living room, but it somehow was clear they had been arranged during a fit of compliance with cultural expectations. We had similar photos in our house, but the arrangement was huge and constantly changing, as our family grew with marriages, new cousins, and in-laws. Dan and I took a small percentage of the photos off the Sweeney wall and secretly exchanged them with all of the photos on the Keefe wall. My sisters reacted immediately, thinking the Keefe photos moderately funny, but wondering when ours would be returned. It was weeks before any of the Keefes noticed or commented.

Our family was conventional and close; I loved seeing the Keefes be unconventional and close.

It had been nine years since I began the process of adopting my three fathers. I was no longer as worried about my potential skills as a father; it felt to me as if the gaping hole I had once sensed in myself was being filled with collected wisdom.

But even in the last months of high school, I still noticed the dads. Many of my friends had great moms who were a steady presence in our lives, but I loved visiting with the dads, whenever they were around. For a few minutes, on a Friday or Saturday night, I would talk to the men when I stopped by to pick up their son on the way to a party or a game.

Mr. McNab, Joey's dad, called me by my surname only.

"Come on in, Sweeney," Mr. McNab would say. "Take off your coat and have a seat. Talk to me." He always had a half smile, as if he didn't quite trust anything I said. But he listened always. "Oh, yeah?" he'd say as he raised his eyebrows, several times over in a single conversation.

Mr. Voreyer was another dad with a half smile, and he also asked questions while rarely offering his own opinion. He, too, was a good listener. Mr. Gillman, Don's dad, was another who called me "Sweeney," but he spoke to me in a way that suggested we were equals, that we were peers. Mr. Hart, Greg's dad, almost never got up from his chair, but was very funny, with an exceptional dry wit. Mr. Renk, Gerard's dad, was reserved, and Mr. Rosenbaum, Rick and Lee's dad, was very smart and very interested in our potential career paths.

I remember, still, the way these men shook hands, the way they stood or sat in their living room, the ways they insisted that we boys come inside for a visit while waiting for their son. There were houses where we avoided the dads, of course, and there were times when we honked the car horn from the street. But more often than not, my friends and I knocked on the doors and stepped inside for a short visit. For my friends, they may have been obligatory exercises in politeness; for me, the visits had genuine meaning, and I was always happy to prolong the conversations. I would be gone soon, away at college, and wanted to enjoy my time with these men before leaving.

My own house was a place where friends would stop in to visit—not just with me, but with the rest of the family. My friends liked my mom, who was someone kids loved to talk to. They respected, as I did, how hard she worked—she had raised six kids on her own, worked at a high school, and now sold hand-sewn crafts at boutiques and fairs around the Bay Area. She made tiny "door hangers," elegant strips of lined fabric about six inches long. On one end, she sewed a loop, for hanging over the door handle; at the other end was a tiny bell, which she imported in bulk from India. The sounds of the sewing machine had long been contemptible for me—audible proof of the unfairness that required my mom to sew all the time just to make ends meet. Now the sewing machine had a partner—the tingling of bells as she sewed them to the fabric. When friends were over, she sat on the couch and continued to sew, the conversation rising above the sound of tiny brass bells. Kathy and Anne were both living at home then—the other three were living on their own—and my friends also liked to talk with both of them.

Although my mom was an adept listener, she and I managed to avoid some of the more challenging conversations for parents and teens. If listening was her best skill and I was hesitant about emotions or emotionally charged subjects, we weren't going to get very far. When I was a senior in high school, she handed me a book, *Dear Eighth Grader,* which explained the process of human reproduction.

"After all these kids, I guess I kind of forgot," she claimed. "I gave this to the other kids when they were in seventh or eighth grade, but I just forgot about all of this with you. Why don't you read it, and you can ask me questions."

I told her I didn't need it at this point and told myself I had learned most of what I needed to know, even though I had yet to put any of it into practice. I was lying to myself and to her, though I didn't quite know it at the time. I found ways to catch up, as people do, but for a long time, that is what it would feel like: catching up.

The consequences of this unwillingness or inability to talk about important things would soon be revealed in other ways as well.

13

After All These Years

We never really talked about him. We didn't tell stories about him, didn't ask about him, and rarely referred to him in conversation. Whenever I did bring him up, I referred to him as "Daddy." It felt strange to be seventeen and calling him Daddy, but it was the only name I had ever used to address him when he was alive; even though I couldn't recall actually saying it to him directly, using any other term felt unnatural. Our pattern of avoidance was by then familiar, so it did not seem unusual to me. I still craved more information about him but lacked the words or the courage to ask questions. I knew I was afraid of sadness—my mother's and my own. I never stopped to think about why it was that the others didn't raise him in conversation. I never stopped to think about whether or not there were other reasons.

It was a Friday night during my last year in high school. Anne was a sophomore at the local junior college and Kathy was a sophomore in high school. We were having dinner with our mother and were joined by Aileen, who was out living on her own. Aileen, in the midst of a series of stories, made a few casual references to drinking: Some friends were drunk at a party one night, and a different group had snuck beers into a Giants' game on another night. The mentions were quick asides, with the drink not central to the story being told.

If there was a buildup to what our mother was about to say—during that meal or in the years before it—I certainly hadn't noticed.

As Aileen finished a story, our mom's face began to contort, looking as if she was trying to mask some great frustration or hurt.

"Why is there always beer?" she asked, and left the question hanging. I didn't have a clue where she was headed. It seemed an unfair question to ask of Aileen, who was dumbstruck.

"Why do you need to have alcohol to have a good time?" Mom asked. She was now crying openly, but her tears did not stop me from being angry with her. I don't recall who stepped up to Aileen's defense first, but Anne, Kathy, and I all struggled to say something. I know I said that Mom was overreacting, that it was just a story.

"Don't you know it's in your blood?" she asked. "Don't you know you need to be careful?" Now Mom was barely able to speak and my own eyes welled up as I sat, riveted and quiet, at the end of the table. I could not say a thing; I could only close my eyes and breathe deeply, trying to stop a flood of tears. I now understood, in an instant, why the topic of Daddy had been avoided for so long.

"Don't you know your father was an alcoholic? Don't you know it means you have to be careful? The tendency is part of you! It's part of this family!"

I don't know who spoke next. If the conversation went on much longer, I was unaware. The only thing I heard, the only thing I held onto, was that my father was an alcoholic. Dead fathers tend to get labeled as saints or deadbeats—with little acknowledgment that most men are neither. My father, though we had talked of him so rarely, had been a saint. The small references from people around town—*your dad was a great guy*—had added up to something; aside from the scars on his chest, he had been, for fourteen years, a man without flaws. Now, he was a deadbeat. I hated him.

It would take many years to sort this out, to know more about why we had kept the topic hidden for so long.

Pat had known but had never said it. He took Mom's lead and tried to run a household that knew more joy than sadness; he was also troubled by a handful of unpleasant memories and by his own anger toward his father. With conversations about our father suppressed or muted, his pleasant memories faded, but the bad ones remained. When these were all he had left of Daddy, Pat didn't want to raise them, even when asked. "I didn't want to bring them up if they were only negative," he would say many years later. No one had given the ten-year-old boy permission to talk. No one had told him that it was okay to be angry, that it might be natural to swirl in a confluence of emotions—anger, sadness, guilt, or relief.

Aileen remembers almost nothing, still, of our daddy. She remembers her guilt, the nineteen steps she did not take. She remembers her anger at Mom, who had told her Daddy would live. And she remembers her guilt for feeling angry at a time of death. No one had given the nine-year-old girl permission to hold such conflicting emotions.

Terry, Anne, Kathy, and I would become occasional detectives, asking questions of relatives, neighbors, and family friends. We did so rarely, and our questions were often indirect, because the topic still seemed forbidden. For a long time, we had doubts about whether or not Mom was telling the truth, about whether or not she was exaggerating our father's affliction.

Terry talked to Pat Ranney, who confirmed that our dad had been a drinker, though she suggested that Mom exaggerated the impact. But Terry also talked to some of our aunts, who denied that our father might have had a weakness; they could not see what others did. Anne's boyfriend at the time admitted to her that he had already heard of our dad's drinking—one of his friend's fathers had worked with our daddy in the city maintenance yard and talked of their getting drunk together. Kathy, who by then had been adopted by nearly all the men on our block, had the neighbors to consult. Several years later, Dolores Kelly would help me understand by saying, "It was all so sad, so hard to watch. First the drinking and then the sickness." The tone of her voice reminded me that he had been through a lot in his short life, that he may have known a great deal of fear.

I find it difficult to judge my mother harshly for failing to talk with us about our father. He died in 1962, and few people then understood what healthy grieving might look like. Few people then understood that sadness could only leave if it was acknowledged. And even the advice from the priest—to bring us to church with a smile—might have had merit. Our family may have been protected by the entire community of San Bruno in part because our mom was an approachable widow. We were not forlorn, despite our relative poverty. It was easy to help us. In hindsight, it seems obvious that we could have struck a balance between private grieving and public accommodation. If only we knew.

It would take many years to reconstruct our image of our father. He had indeed been an alcoholic, but we began to hear stories about him that would place that one-word description in context. Alice Gaffney would tell me that all of Mom's friends loved him the most, that he was the one they were most thrilled to have joining their group. Helen Barry's brother-in-law told me of pranks our daddy would play on his mother, on stern Grandma Sweeney. Our Auntie Anne talked of his years in the navy, of how he was always so protective of his little sisters, of how he could dance. She talked of his laughter.

We had always been told that he was very smart, but I recall the night, when we were all adults—all of us were older, even, than our father had ever been—we discovered the program saved from his high school graduation. On the front cover was a list of twenty or so boys who graduated from St. Ignatius with "highest honors." The first inside page listed boys who graduated with "distinction," and the opposite page had others who graduated with "honors." Our father was not on these lists, so we assumed the program was from the wrong year. But on the back, there were more names, and one of them was James Joseph Sweeney. These fellows were listed simply, perhaps graciously, as "graduates."

"It was a good thing he could dance," I said aloud, laughing.

My mother protested, blaming his academic showing on rheumatic fever and the fact that it forced him to transfer high schools. But I clung lovingly to the notion that Daddy was ordinary. It was evidence that my father was neither saint nor deadbeat. I now had a father I could tease, even after his death, even after all these years. It had taken time, but I could now see that so many people had been right, that my father was a good man. It felt good to finally understand that. I wish I had seen him dance.

14

Three Fathers

In the spring of my senior year in high school, I was accepted at Berkeley. Though the school was just a forty-minute drive from our house, I was definitely going away to college. I had already saved enough money to pay for my first full year. I would live on campus and would come home only on occasional weekends and over breaks.

I would soon be turning eighteen and knew that the big green checks from the Department of the Treasury would start to be addressed in my name. Social Security benefits intended for the young children of a deceased parent go directly to the surviving parent. But when the children turn eighteen, the checks begin going to them, so long as they remain in school. When Pat turned eighteen and was heading off to college, he simply signed over the checks and gave them to Mom. His logic was simple. Marian Sweeney was a widow with young children and needed help. Pat Sweeney, her son, was now a grown man and could take care of himself. I don't know how many people, inside our family or outside of it, knew he had done so. Anne and I were the two others to graduate from four-year colleges; both of us followed Pat's lead. In my case, the checks were big enough that my "income" was such that I could not qualify for financial aid scholarships. Still, my pride in being able to stand on my own was greater than any jealousies I might have felt then. I taught my mom how to forge my signature, and she would do so each month, using the funds to keep our house afloat.

In April, a girl invited me to the Mercy High School Senior Ball. I had been away on a trip to Washington, D.C., when Crestmoor's big dance was held, so this was it: my high school swan song. It would be a special evening, with dinner at a restaurant—still a novel event for me—and dancing in San Francisco. Parties would extend late into the evening and early morning, so there was no curfew on this night; my mom trusted me, and four o'clock in the morning, or even later, would be acceptable. I simply had to promise not to drive drunk, a promise I kept.

It was on a Saturday, and after leaving the deli early at three o'clock in the afternoon, I used the family car to pick up my rented tuxedo.

When I returned home from the rental shop, Chick Kelly was waiting at our front door.

He was there with George Schaumeffel, an old family friend whose late wife, Paulette, had been a close friend to Auntie Anne and to my mom. They dropped by, unannounced, to help me get dressed. I took a shower and shaved, though I most likely didn't need to do the latter. As I stood in my room in my boxers, the two men acted as valets. George unzipped the plastic bag from the rental shop, laying the garments neatly on the bed, taking his time in doing so. After I put on the white shirt with layers of pressed fabric on the placket, he set the black buttons in place. Chick brushed the patent leather shoes with his sleeve, and the three of us talked as I slowly and deliberately dressed and was dressed. George buttoned the suspenders to the back of my pants, and each man took a strap, pulling it over my shoulders, fumbling with the buttons as they affixed them in the front. I held my arms out as they inserted cuff links, and held my arms up as they wrapped the cummerbund. I felt their hands on my stomach and shoulders as they turned me this way and that, much as a barber does while cutting hair. There was teasing and banter, and talk of dances they had been to long ago. It was a nice and long conversation, with Chick interrupting occasionally to say, "You look great. You look great."

I took forever to lace up the shoes, not wanting the moment to pass, this moment when men were doting on me and acknowledging some rite of passage. I sat on the edge of my bed for a long time, as they leaned against the walls and kept talking. It felt as if none of us wanted the conversation to wane. As they helped me slip on the dark blue tuxedo jacket with the black lapels, Chick said it again, "You look great." He shook his head as he did so, implying, to me at least, that so much time had passed, that so much had happened.

We talked with my mom in the living room, and she took

a photo of the three men—George, Chick, and me. I kissed her good-bye and then hugged George. When I hugged Chick, he held me close and told me to have fun. He again said I looked great.

A few weeks later, Chick was diagnosed with an advanced stage of bladder cancer. He was told he had six months to live. The strongest man I knew now had a body that would quickly be ravaged by illness.

Neil Kelly, Rick Garban, and I, along with a few others, spent a week camping in Yosemite that summer. Every day, or what seemed like every day, Neil walked from the campground to a pay phone and called home. I could see him from a distance, holding the phone to one ear and leaning his head against the glass booth. I checked his eyes as he walked back toward us, not wanting to ask, but needing to know how his father was. Chick was holding up, and he would last a full eighteen months before giving in.

He had suffered two bouts of cancer earlier in life, the first time when he was thirty-five, but none of us kids knew that. This time, his doctors tried radiation, but they found its impact on his lymph system was so severe that it caused more trouble than it was worth. There would be no stopping the illness, and the only issue became how they would manage his pain. It turned out, not surprisingly, that he took pain well, or at least he suffered through it with little complaint and without imposing on others.

He simply held on, stretching out his pain and his life, for as long as he possibly could. He stayed around long enough to let everyone say their good-byes. And, if it hadn't been said quite right, he stayed around long enough to give people a few more tries. He stayed around long enough to listen. Most of the time, he was in bed or in a recliner in the back room at the Kellys' house, away from the noise if he needed to sleep, away from distractions if someone wanted to talk.

He was unafraid of death, a cliché used for many, but a genuine reality for him. He didn't complain of the unfairness, but instead talked of his faith, of how he wanted to find out what God had in store for him—in life and in death. He had a mission, to show us that death was simply a part of life, that there was peace in a willingness to accept whatever challenges God presented, that life didn't really end when humans died. He was open about all of this. His faith was so obvious, so clear, that the priests at St. Timothy's sent a stream of young deacons over to the Kellys, so they could see the dying man. If one part of their future role as priests was to console the dying and those left behind, Chick would be a good teacher. I only heard these stories and never saw the deacons myself, but I picture timid young men, their eyes red with anticipatory tears as they came in, leaving after a full meal, a few drinks, and a long conversation that started with Chick chewing them out for being so damn morose.

I was now away at school and visited him only once during his final months. He was gaunt, pale, and in obvious decline, but his smile and hands looked unchanged to me. He said very little, I assume because he was wracked with pain, and I said very little, afraid that once I really spoke, once the tears began to roll, there would be no stopping, of either words or tears. I did manage to say I was thankful for all he had done for my mom, and for all he had done for my family. I said there were things he had said to me that were very helpful, that had played a big role in my life.

To fill the silence and stave off the tears, I also blurted out, "And thanks for all that meat!" I laid my hand on his and said I would see him again soon.

I was no more prepared to say good-bye to Chick than I had been when I was three and my own father had died. I had grown in many ways since Daddy's death, but not in the way that would help me say what I felt most deeply. Too much remained bottled up inside me. I don't regret that I could not find the words to be more precise, to tell him exactly what I was feeling, to tell him that he had shown me how to do the one thing, to be the one thing, that might someday be what mattered most. I simply wasn't ready.

His pain was so great that, by the time of his death, there was a tinge of relief—he had done more, and offered more, than we could have expected, even from him. He was only fifty and the father of nine children, some of whom were still quite young. While his death was horribly sad, it somehow seems reasonable to say that it was also beautiful. He was a powerful figure, even in death, but beauty is what comes to mind when I think of his passing.

At his funeral, the church was packed, as it had been for my own daddy's funeral. Chick's was the first modern funeral I attended, where the form was determined not by rote, but was a creative expression of love by those who had loved him the most. Some of the songs expressed sadness; others called forth images of a smiling Chick. We sang "Side by Side," "Oh Happy Day," and "The Battle Hymn of the Republic." At the offering of the gifts, his children brought forth mementos of Chick: his butcher knives, a bottle of Scotch, a photo of Dolores and him on vacation. It was a genuine celebration of the fact that he had lived, and of the manner in which he had lived.

We went back to the Kellys' house after the evening rosary, standing in the room where Chick died or sitting again at the massive dining room table, at the spot where he had spoken so directly to me. The Sweeneys joined the Kellys and many others at Chick's gravesite the next morning, staying with them until his body was lowered into the grounds of the same cemetery where our own father was buried. I had never been to a burial before and was deeply touched when Neil asked if we would be there with them.

What I was not able to say to Chick, I was able to say to both Sherm Heaney and Jim Gaffney.

I was in my late twenties, living on the East Coast and working as press secretary to Senator Gary Hart, when Sherm came down with viral meningitis. His body temperature rose and plummeted for several days, and there were moments when he lost control of his speech. He could say the words, but they came out in the wrong order; he was speaking backward. Once his doctors confirmed that he had not had a stroke, that it was indeed viral meningitis, they kept him in the hospital for two days, then sent him home, having given him aspirin and nothing more. Of the different varieties of meningitis, the viral form is the least dangerous. But it was a scare nonetheless.

When I heard the news, I wrote a short note to Sherm to tell him of the role he had played and explained the key lesson I had learned from him. He called to thank me, though he spent most of the call reassuring me about his health. He was gracious, but downplayed his role. He said he felt as if he had done nothing special but was pleased if I had learned from him. It seemed he was embarrassed by the attention, as if he didn't want to be singled out on his own. Perhaps he sees parenting as a team sport.

He and Dee still live in San Bruno, they still see my mother at St. Robert's, and my siblings who live on the peninsula still see him around town. He hasn't aged in twenty years.

When I was in my thirties, my siblings and I hosted a retirement party for our mother, then in her midsixties and finally quitting her job at Burlingame High School. I knew that Jim Gaffney had been having heart trouble, and I was looking forward to seeing him. It had been a long, long time since I had looked to him for any lessons or guidance; I simply wanted to check in on him. He and Alice were out on a balcony, talking with a small group, when I joined them. Jim and I separated off into our own conversation, and he once again made a point of saying how much he admired my mother—we were there, after all, to honor her that day. As he said this, so much came back to me, and I began to tell him about the role he had played in my life.

I told him of my plan to find three fathers, of how I had chosen him and why. I told him some of the things I had learned from him, one of which was that a good man respected women. He was stunned—it was unfair to tell him in public, I then realized—and he worked hard to fight back tears. That was not an unusual response for him.

"I had no idea," he said, over and over, as he closed his eyes and shook his head. "I had no idea." Alice had managed to hear part of our conversation and beamed with pride as she slid in next to him, putting her arm through his. Jim seemed to let the idea settle in, and he, too, began to smile.

"I really loved your dad," Jim said, looking directly at me now. "He was a great guy, and it means a lot to me that I was able to help."

We talked a bit about Tahoe, yard work, and *Tora! Tora! Tora!* It was the last time I saw him; a year later, he died during heart surgery.

The strategy I devised when I was eight had worked. Three men, fathers I had chosen, had given me confidence. I would enter fatherhood no less prepared than other men. I would become a father knowing there were experiences, particular moments, I could rely on when I needed help.

I suppose the strategy could have backfired. I could have picked the wrong men, I could have invested too much hope in them, I could have wandered off into a fantasy and been let down by men who knew nothing of my hopes or expectations. But that didn't happen. The three men I chose helped me greatly. And they had help, because others shaped me as well—my brother, my grandfather, my uncles, Paul at the deli, Tommy Lara, the men on Cypress Avenue, and so many others in San Bruno.

Perhaps because what I sought was so obvious, the lessons I took from each of the fathers were also obvious.

———————————————

Sherm Heaney taught that the first rule of being a dad was to show up. He was always there. I now catch myself smiling, even laughing to myself, at my stepdaughter Hannah's water polo games. I can't stop myself from commenting on the good passes, on the steals, on the girls who cut toward the goal at precisely the right moment. I say things for Hannah, and I say things for the other girls. "Nice pass, Tanya," I'll hear myself saying, and I'll have waited until the crowd is quiet and Tanya knows that more than the goal is being celebrated. My mother reminded me recently that when I explained to her why I took myself out of the running for a job in the White House—this was when I was getting married and would become a stepfather to Hannah—I had a simple way of putting it: It's what Sherm Heaney would have done.

Jim Gaffney taught me about respect and generosity—and

also of the value of getting kids out of the house. I recall a night several years back when my wife, Jennifer, went to visit her best friend from childhood, Nancy Anton, a single mother of four girls. When I saw how much Jennifer and Nancy wanted a quiet visit together, my role was obvious. I loaded Nancy's four girls into the minivan, took them all to the movies, and found an ice cream parlor afterward. I had a great time and thought of Jim throughout the evening. If I had worn a cardigan sweater that night, I would have fastened only the bottom two buttons in his honor.

Chick Kelly taught me about strength and steadiness. There have been many times during my years as a parent when I've felt the need to raise difficult topics at home. When I've been able to do so, it is often because I think of Chick before speaking—I can see him very clearly. That image is what helps me sit down at the table and talk it out. I'm not as good at it as he was, but he gave me a target, a sense of how it's done. I try to assume some of his strength if I find myself wavering. And Chick's influence may be the deepest and the most lasting: He showed me how to die.

Now, more than thirty-five years after adopting them as my own, I'm still conscious of these men, and the lessons they taught me. My life has been different from the lives they led as young men. They all stayed close to home, took jobs that allowed them to put family first, and became reliable and important figures in their neighborhoods and parishes. I moved across and around the country several times. I took jobs in academia, as a television reporter, and as an environmental and political activist—all jobs that can lead to the postponement, or ruination, of families. I followed my ambitions and served on a national level, as a presidential appointee, working directly with members of the president's cabinet and, on occasion, with the president. But I do rely on these men, still. A few years back, I hit a period when I felt I needed help, as a father and as a husband, and I asked the three wives to send me photos of their men. I wanted a framed image of the three fathers, right there on my dresser, as a point of reference, as a reminder.

There were many times growing up when I felt unfettered without a father of my own. I felt relief that there was no family profession for which I might be destined, that there was no one man whose satisfaction mattered as much as, if not more than, my own. I believed it allowed me to develop my own ambitions, to find something that was truly mine, done for reasons that were truly my own. If there was destiny in my life, it was rooted in the big green checks from the U.S. Department of the Treasury—the only career I ever imagined for myself was one of public service, one in which I could give back to a country that had given me so much.

Though I found this independence to be a strength, I also know that the stability and confidence I gained from my father figures—and the many others who helped them—paved the way for any successes. I watched these men, studied them, and leaned on them. And they showed me how. I am grateful.

Epilogue:
Learning to Speak

My brother, Pat, called me one afternoon in the summer between my junior and senior years at Berkeley. It was July 1979.

He got straight to the point: He had just been told he had a brain tumor. He said the doctor was optimistic, that the tumor was likely benign, but that he needed to undergo brain surgery within a week. The doctor also told him to get his affairs in order, an indirect way of saying my brother should prepare, logistically and financially at least, for his own death. He was twenty-seven.

I went to his house as soon as I could, finding him quite calm. He was relieved, in a sense, that the dizziness that plagued him for months was not an inner ear infection—which could last a lifetime and would cost him his job as a firefighter. Now, with a brain tumor, it would be cured or he would be gone, and the certainty had its appeal. He was also relieved because another great concern had been addressed just before I arrived at his house. Nearly all of his medical leave time had been used up during tests at doctors' offices and hospitals, but a successful surgery would still have him out of work for three more months; the loss of his job was a very real possibility. But Joe Schaukowitz, one of Pat's classmates from St. Robert's and a San Bruno firefighter himself, had just come by to tell Pat that all of his shifts had been covered. The fire department staff started a phone tree as soon as they heard the news, with each man volunteering to cover a number of Pat's shifts. Within a few hours, they had someone assigned to each of Pat's scheduled shifts for the next three months. Pat was to focus on getting well; they would take care of the fires. He would live, they said, and he would remain in the department.

On the night before his surgery, I visited him at Kaiser Hospital; I think this was the night I brought him dinner from Taco Bell. I don't remember what we talked about, but I do know that I could not say what I knew I should say, what I wanted to say. I could not thank him, nor could I tell him I loved him. I could not talk about fears or hopes or the things we had been through together. I still did not have the words. The language used to describe deeply felt emotions was still a foreign one to me, and probably to him. We couldn't say much of anything that mattered, though the fact that I was there, with him and for him, was a statement he could see as well as anyone.

His surgery, scheduled for six hours, took eight. Aileen, who never left the waiting room, still describes it as the longest day of her life. They drilled four holes in the back of our brother's skull, removed a large section of the bone, and used scalpels and vacuums guided by microscopes to remove what the doctor described as a vascular lesion, a benign tumor, the size of a golf ball. Dr. Cecil Jun walked into the waiting room to find Pat's wife, Ellen, all of his siblings, his aunts, and a few family friends. He looked exhausted, completely worn down by the stress of holding a life in his hands.

"The surgery went about as well as we could possibly hope," Dr. Jun said. "We got it all. It's not been tested yet, but I'm certain it's benign. He's gonna be okay. He'll be fine. He'll be in the hospital for another ten days or so and probably out of work for maybe three months. But he's gonna be fine. He's gonna be fine."

We were delirious. We hugged and shouted and cried and made plans to head back to San Bruno for a big dinner together. I stayed behind, because I drove separately, and looked around for Mom. I looked in the main waiting room, which we had taken over for most of the day, and didn't see her there. I looked in a smaller waiting room and then another, and that was where I saw her.

My mother was hunched over in her chair, and she was sobbing.

"Why couldn't Jim have lived?" she said to no one. "Why couldn't Jim have lived?" It was like the Curran wedding all over again—at the height of joy, she became lost in a maze of emotions, unable to find stable ground.

My brother would live. But here was Mom crying over the man, the dancer, who did not.

What I would learn in the coming days was that so much

of the experience had been familiar to my mom. Both men—her husband and her son—worked for the city of San Bruno. Both were in danger of losing their jobs because of lengthy illnesses, and both had friends who stepped in to cover shifts. Both were young fathers—Pat's son Michael took his first steps while his daddy was in the hospital. At seven o'clock on the weekday mornings leading up to Pat's surgery and our daddy's, there were dozens of people at St. Robert's, dozens of friends, attending mass to pray for a Sweeney in danger. And then there were the phone calls, from people calling to ask of his condition or to express their concern. Mom stood there for much of the week before Pat's surgery, in that spot between the dining room and kitchen, with one hand on her hip and one on the phone—over and over, as she had done once before. All of it, especially the phone calls, was too much for our mother.

She spent most of that summer at home, and those of us who were living with her then kept her away from the phone. We screened her calls, asked friends to send notes instead, and watched and waited as our mother wavered between the thrill of her son's recovery and her grief over her husband's death. More than anyone, Kathy watched over our mother.

It wasn't a challenge to extract the lessons. It had been seventeen and a half years, and she had never taken time to grieve. She was a mother, the mother of six, and had given every ounce of her energy to her children. But the need to grieve would not go away, not until the grieving had occurred. And the decision to be happy, to smile for the public, simply prolonged the inevitable.

It was a breakthrough—a painful breakthrough—for our mother and for the rest of us. Once I saw my mom talk openly of her own sorrow, of how much she missed him, of how deeply in love the two of them had been and how unfair it all was, only then did I begin to develop an ear for a language I had not yet learned. And if the language was new, the lessons it could teach were still elusive. I could watch my three father figures to see what it was that men did, to see how fathers acted. But how men might handle their feelings—and what I felt, as a boy and as a young man—still needed exploration.

When I was thirty-eight years old, the age my father was when he died, I, too, was a young father. Hannah, my stepdaughter since she was seven, was ten. Julia, our youngest, was one. I had just had minor surgery, and the doctor's instructions for my recovery were simple: Stay in bed for two days and don't lift anything heavier than a football for three days.

As I lay awake in bed later that day, Julia ran to me for comfort. She was upset about something—I don't recall what—and was crying in the way kids do when they are more frustrated than hurt. She wanted me to hold her, to pull her close to my chest, to rock her back and forth in a rhythm that was ours alone. But holding her then was not something I could do. I could not reach down to pick up my daughter; I could not give her the physical comfort she desired. My words of explanation meant nothing to her, and she herself did not have words to explain her feelings. She wanted Daddy to hold her, and Daddy could not or would not.

It struck me right then that I had been in this place before. I saw in Julia the desperation of a young child, of a child who craves, but will not find, the comfort that only one person can provide. It was me that I was seeing. My daddy in bed, with the scar across his chest and back, too frail and weak to pick up his boy, too worn out, even, for a hug. All these years later, I realized it was not just my mother's sadness and pain that might percolate to the surface, or my siblings', but my own. For so long, I had assumed our father's death was much harder on my brother and sisters—they were older, they knew him, they had memories, I told myself, so of course it was harder for them.

And there was the August day two years later, when Julia was three and a half years old, exactly the age I was when my father died. I drove home to Ojai after a day at work, and there she was on the front porch. There she was jumping up and down, smiling and waving at me, the only man in the world who mattered right then. As I parked the car and walked up the driveway, she ran toward me, her arms wide open. And she said the words I must have said so long ago.

"Daddy, Daddy, Daddy, Daddy!"

It was the most joyous sound I have ever heard—a young child so madly in love. As I scooped her up in my arms, I finally understood that I, too, had loved my daddy that much. Thirty-eight years had passed—as long as my father's lifetime—and I now understood something I had forgotten so long ago. I loved him. And I missed him.

I found other fathers who would help me on the path to manhood and fatherhood. But I still missed my daddy. Knowing that, and saying it aloud, helped me feel whole.

Acknowledgments

Many people helped me while writing this book, and I remain grateful to all of them.

My mother, Marian Sweeney, allowed me to publicly explore issues that are often difficult to discuss, even privately. She was open, as she has been throughout my adult life, about her motives and reasons for acting and continues, to this day, to seek lessons and meaning in the events we shared. Most important, her strength and skill as a mother when I was young gave me the stability and confidence to search for father figures.

Salon.com ran the brief essay that led to a call from the publisher of this book, Judith Regan. Salon remains (hopefully, it remains!) the most thoughtful, interesting, and engaging place on the Internet. (Full disclosure: My wife is a longtime Salon employee.)

Cassie Jones, my editor at ReganBooks, convinced me to take on this project. She gently and sagely steered me along the path from outline to finished manuscript.

The Kelly, Gaffney, and Heaney families provided support

and encouragement and took time to speak with me about their own memories of these events. Several of the kids (all of them now adults) reviewed the manuscript along the way. Reconnecting with them through this project has been a joy.

Michael Reese and Dan Keefe reviewed the manuscript and provided helpful editorial guidance. I appreciate their help, and their friendship.

My aunt, Anne Desler, helped me greatly by holding on to images of her brother—my father—long enough to help me begin seeing who he really was.

My siblings—Pat Sweeney, Aileen Kerr, Terry Walsh, Anne de la Rosa, and Kathy Fitzpatrick—each reviewed several drafts and provided helpful edits and insights. I'm grateful for their help. I'm also grateful for the fact that we still get along, still see one another often, and still roll our eyes and laugh at the same stories.

Most important, my wife, Jennifer Foote Sweeney, provided immeasurable support, as well as superb editorial advice. I am grateful to her for both—and for much more.